SS7 – The Quiet Revolution That Changed Your Telephone Service

by Ralph Harvey

SS7 – The Quiet Revolution That Changed Your Telephone
Service
by Ralph Harvey

Subject headings:

Computers & Technology | Networking | Telephony

Published in the United States of America.

Table of Contents

Dedication

This mini-book is dedicated to the men and women, many of whom I know, who faithfully serve the public as telecommunications professionals. These individuals work at landline and cellular telephone companies, hardware and software vendors, universities and their research affiliates, federal agencies and commissions, The Internet Society (including the Internet Engineering Task Force), The Institute of Electrical and Electronic Engineers, Inc. (IEEE), and other professional organizations. They generally work quietly and outside the public view, but their efforts have a substantial impact on public safety, convenience, and the quality of our lives.

A Note To Readers

Signaling System 7, along with its international variations, has billions of stakeholders, and not just engineers, technicians, or telecommunications executives. Virtually everyone who uses any kind of telephone or data device on a telecommunications network is affected by SS7, as the system is commonly referred to in the United States. Not only is SS7 vital for the functioning of these networks; it directly affects the quality and cost of your voice and data telephone service. Unfortunately, this topic is almost completely unknown to the public. In fact, SS7 could easily be mistaken for a top-secret military or intelligence program by many people. Since the widespread dissemination of information is long overdue, it is a pleasure to introduce you to the behind-the-scenes system that has bettered your life in so many ways.

In writing about this fascinating subject, the plan is to present SS7 in a way that will be of interest to a wide variety of readers. So this is not a technical book for network engineers or software developers; there are other texts for that. In fact, what you are about to read is really a mini-book, the non-fiction equivalent of a novella. Despite the fact that this is not a textbook for future technicians or engineers, it will provide a "lite" introduction to selected telecommunications topics. Those who develop an interest in this topic can then delve more deeply in one of the fine technically oriented books on signaling systems and related topics.

To make this story of SS7 interesting for a wide audience of readers, it begins with a historical perspective. That makes it easier to see how and why telephony – the technology of telephone systems – and its scientific underpinnings, developed. So we journey back in time to before Alexander Graham Bell's 1876 telephone patent was issued, and cover the salient topics in a way that most readers without a technical background will understand. But this is not just a history; you will learn quite a bit about telephone systems, communication networks, and important details of how Signaling System 7 actually works. At the end of some sections there are side notes about selected topics. You can skim past these notes if you choose, but many of you – especially high school or college students with an interest in science or technology – might enjoy them.

For those of you who are contemplating your career, serving as a high school guidance counselor or working as a faculty advisor at a college, having even a little knowledge of SS7 may point you towards some unexpected options. The design and operation of telecommunications networks, along with the activities of component and service vendors, all provide interesting jobs and career opportunities. Besides engineers and technicians, these companies also need people with non-technical expertise such as accountants, marketing experts, attorneys, and a plethora of other skill sets. Having some awareness and knowledge about SS7 might give you a competitive advantage in a job interview, either with a telecom or one of their hundreds of vendors. To those young adult readers who are contemplating a stint in the armed forces, you might want to consider enlisting for a Military Occupational Specialty (MOS) in electronics, radar, avionics, signal encryption or data links. These military specialties can get you training and assignments that bring enormous satisfaction, and transfer nicely into civilian careers in telecommunications. And some of you may want nothing more than a better understanding of how your telephone service provider operates. That's important too.

One of the great benefits of modern technology is that it enables an author with an important story or message to communicate with so many readers. As an adjunct instructor at a community college, I could reach out to as many as twenty students in my classroom, or maybe as many as forty in any given semester. Now, useful knowledge can be quickly and economically conveyed over the Internet to many thousands of deserving readers. So wherever you are, and whatever your interests or situation, I hope that this look at Signaling System 7 will give you some useful and enjoyable reading. In the final analysis, SS7 is not just about telephone network technology; it's about you.

Notice and Disclaimer

This literary work is intended to provide general information and a historical overview to a wide audience with diversion backgrounds. It is not intended, and should not be used, as engineering or other professional guidance. The services of a registered professional engineer or other properly qualified professional or vendor should be used when such knowledge or services are required.

Acknowledgements

A literary work is a product that represents much more than the thoughts and words of an author. Especially in nonfiction, a book or mini-book is the result of many influences and contributors. So it is with a deep sense of gratitude that this author acknowledges the following organizations and individuals whose important contributions made this mini-book about SS7 possible.

The Federal Communications Commission (FCC), in addition to being an independent regulatory agency, plays a crucial role in telecommunications. In addition to the mandates of the Telecommunications Act of 1996, the FCC is responsible for such matters as public safety and homeland security. Consumers benefit from the actions of its Consumer and Government Affairs Bureau (CGB), Wireless telecommunications Services (WCS) and the Wireline Competition Bureau (WCB). The FCC also archives records that are invaluable to researchers, and for which this author is most grateful. The FCC website is: http://www.fcc.gov.

The Institute of Electrical and Electronic Engineers, Inc. (IEEE) has been instrumental in engendering research, dissemination of knowledge, and the publication of books and papers that pertain to telecommunications. IEEE has also been at the forefront of establishing important telecommunications standards such as 802.11. Just to cite one example, in 2007 an IEEE task group began the process of "rolling up" many of the predecessor 802.11 standards, which then became known as IEEE 802.11-2012. A special thanks is extended to Dean Masters at the IEEE History Center for assistance in searching IEEE documents. IEEE headquarters is located in New York City, and their historical and publications offices are located in Piscataway, New Jersey. Readers are encouraged to visit the IEEE's official website at http://www.ieee.org.

The International Telecommunications Union (ITU) is an affiliate of the United Nations, and is based in Geneva, Switzerland. The organization dates back to 1865, when it began as the International telegraph Union. In 1947, the organization became affiliated with the relatively new United Nations in 1947, and was renamed the International Telegraph and Telephone Consultative Committee

(CCITT) in 1956. It them morphed into the ITU in 1993. Of particular interest is that portion that deals with standardization, or ITU-T. The CCITT and the ITU-T played important roles in the early development of SS7, and its international equivalents. Readers may visit the ITU website at: http://www.itu.int/en/Pages/default.aspx.

The Internet Engineering Task Force (IETF) serves The Internet Society and Internet users with a cadre of engineers and supporting entities that work in collaboration to develop and improve the Internet. The IETF operates with an open, transparent process to develop a consensus based on the experience and judgment of the engineering participants. Working papers and drafts evolved into documents called "Request For Comments," or RFCs. This is a rich source of information for anyone who wishes to follow the development of Internet standards and protocols. For example, RFC 3935 (October 2004) provides the IETF mission statement. Readers are encouraged to visit the website of this standards organization at: www.ietf.org. At the time of this publication, the IETF is chaired by Russ Hously, an expert in Internet security and the author of over forty RFCs. Readers are encouraged to visit the IETF website at http://www.ietf.org.

Corporate Archivist William D. "Bill" Caughlin at the AT&T Archives and History Center in San Antonio, Texas was extremely helpful in locating images of the late Dr. Claude E. Shannon of Bell Telephone Laboratories, as well as images of Crossbar and ESS switches that were used by AT&T long lines and the Regional Bell Operating Companies (RBOCs). He also located the images of the telephone operator and the woman speaking on the telephone that appear on the cover, and was able to arrange for use permission for this publication. Thanks to Bill's efforts, these important historical images can be shared with you and other readers.

Dr. Dina Katabi, Professor of Electrical Engineering and Computer Science at the Massachusetts Institute of Technology and co-director of the MIT's Center for Wireless Networks and Mobile Computing, kindly granted permission to use an excerpt of her words in the Epilogue. Professor Katabi, along with colleagues Haitham Hassanieh, Piotr Indyk, and Eric Price, was recognized for work on developing a faster Fourier transform. Professor Katabi has also been a principal investigator in the areas of Random Access Heterogeneous MIMO Networks, IMDShield (securing implantable medical devices), and secure in-band wireless pairing. Any reader with an interest in wireless telecommunications may find it extremely useful to follow the research activities at MIT's Center for Wireless Networks and Mobile Computing. You can visit the official website at: http://wireless.csail.mit.edu/research.

Travis Russell, the author of several important books on telecommunications, kindly reviewed my treatment of SS7. With over thirty years of field engineering and management experience with companies such as Pacific Telephone, United Technologies Switching and Tekelec, he is one of the world's leading authorities on Signaling System 7 and related technologies. I became acquainted with Travis through his books *Telecommunication Protocols* and *Signaling System 7* (Fifth Edition). More recently, he has authored *The IP Multimedia Subsystem (IMS): Session Control and Other Network Operations*, and *Session Initiated Protocol (SIP): Controlling Convergent Networks*, all published by McGraw-Hill. I have always put Travis in the same category as the late Dr. Louis Brown, author of the classic book *A Radar History of World War II: Technical and Military Imperatives*. These are all great reads, and have inspired many careers in avionics and telecommunications. Fortunately, Travis is well and very active from his home in North Carolina.

Dr. Craig Wills is a Professor of Computer Science and head of the Computer Science Department at Worcester Polytechnic Institute. Along with WPI graduate student Can Tatar, Prof. Wills conducted new research on Internet privacy, and kindly granted permission to quote from the Abstract of their report, which is entitled 'Understanding What They Do With What They Know.' In addition to teaching, Professor Wills conducts research in the areas of Internet applications performance and privacy, and has been published extensively. A lengthy partial list of his publications can be viewed at: http://web.cs.wpi.edu/~cew/papers.

College Archivist Ken Grossi at the Oberlin College Archives (in Oberlin, Ohio) was most helpful in locating the image of Elisha Gray and granting use permission. Gray's work in telecommunications is important and not properly recognized, and this author is grateful for

Ken's help.

Photo Historian Heather Moore at the U.S. Senate Historical Office kindly located a digital image of the late Senator William B. Saxbe, and arranged for use permission. Saxbe served as a U.S. senator from Ohio until his appointment as the 70th U.S. attorney general by President Richard M. Nixon. Heathers prompt and efficient handling of this request is very much appreciated.

Finding a usable image of the late U.S. District Judge Harold H. Greene was also a priority, and Research Historian Jake Kobrick at the Federal Judicial Center kindly performed an initial search at the FJC Archives. Linda Ferren of the Historical Society of the District of Columbia Circuit was then able to locate and provide a fine image of Judge Greene in the historical society's archives, and the family of Judge Greene provided an additional image. Thanks also to Ruth Gordon for assisting in the file transfers. The images of Judge Greene that are courtesy of the Greene family and the Historical Society of the D.C. Circuit. This author is very grateful for all of their help.

Mary Harper of Access Points Indexing did the bulk of the proofreading, and provided compelling evidence that authors need careful supervision. In addition, Mary graciously took time away from her busy schedule as an indexer to help keep this project on track. You can visit Mary's website at: accesspointsindexing.com.

Haydee A. Peralta of HNA Design Services provided CAD/D renderings of the SS7 and SIGTRAN protocol stacks, link configurations and other network details. Haydee even provided on popular CAD/D programs, which this author very much appreciates.

Kelly M. Green used her graphic design skills to provide the cover layout. A University of Akron graduate, Kelly also produces cover and interior graphics for Portland Book Review, and proved that she is quite capable of working with artistically challenged authors. Her attention to detail is much appreciated.

M. Chris Johnson, Editor-in-Chief of Portland Book Review, made time in her busy schedule to assist as my literary editor. In particular, Chris was able to provide this author with extremely useful guidance about keeping technical subjects within the grasp of non-technical readers. That was not an easy task, and her patience and understanding are very much appreciated. Readers might enjoy the Portland Book Review website at: www.portlandbookreview.com.

Of course, over the years many friends and former colleagues at Verizon Wireless, especially in technical support and network operations, have impressed me with their dedication and professionalism. That has especially been true on occasions when hurricanes and other forms of severe weather passed through a region. During those periods "all hands on deck" are needed to identify outage locations and restore service as quickly as possible. So if in discussing their efforts this author is not completely impartial, hopefully readers will understand.

Finally, and despite the guidance of others, it is always possible that an author might fail to correct every error or omission prior to publication. Any such failures are the sole responsibility of this author, who hereby apologizes for any errors or omissions that might still exist.

Ralph Harvey
December 2012

Prologue

Access to the local exchange is essential for all interexchange carriers and, as the evidence in the AT&T action has suggested, there are many ways in which the company controlling the local exchange monopoly could discriminate against competitors in the interexchange market.

> – U.S. District Judge Harold H. Greene, in his Modification of Final Judgment, August 24, 1982, in the case of the United States of America, Plaintiff, v. American Telephone and Telegraph Company, et al., Defendants. Civ. A No. 74-1698. 82-0192. Misc. No. 82-0025(PI).[1]

It was Tuesday, April 27th, and arriving fans at Atlanta-Fulton County Stadium were ready for midweek baseball. Early in the season, both the Atlanta Braves and the San Francisco Giants had hopes for the new season – as did their players. The prior season the Braves finished with a lackluster 76-86 record, some 26 games behind the league leading Cincinnati Reds. Much of the fan's hope rested on right fielder Hank Aaron, wearing number 44. Just the day before Aaron hit his 599th career home run, and was looking for number 600. He was ready, and had the confidence of the fans.

Giant's pitcher Gaylord Perry was also confidant, masterful with his pitches, and (in the opinion of many) arrogant. Perry was famous for throwing spitballs, his unique "puffball," and for antics that tended to either bewilder or infuriate batters, managers and even umpires. He was also surrounded by formidable teammates, including such Giant greats as Willy Mays and Willy McCovey. In the first inning Aaron made contact, hitting Perry's pitch off the wall for a double but missing the coveted home run. In their second faceoff of the day, Perry's delivery seemed flawless. But once again Aaron was on it, driving a high fly ball up and over the left-center field fence. Home run number 600 was in the baseball history books, a superb beginning to the 1971 baseball season.

Singer Carole King was also having a good month. Her new studio album Tapestry had just been released by Ode Records, and both It's Too Late and I Feel the Earth Move were quickly climbing the charts. In less than two more months the twenty-nine year old singer-songwriter would watch her album hit number one on the charts, eventually selling some 25 million copies. King's music, along with songs by Gordon Lightfoot, Rod Stewart and Donny Osmond permeated the AM radio airwaves. Records were available on vinyl LPs and 45 discs, but CDs were a decade away. People were also more isolated. Cellphones in any form did not exist, and were not envisioned. But as with the Ramblers, Chevy Corsairs and Ford Falcons that were parked outside Fulton County Stadium, telephone service as it existed in 1971 was coming to an end.

Unlike the Vietnam War or the coming political drama of Watergate, the Quiet Revolution that would affect everyone's telephone service would be almost completely unnoticed. The technologies that affected telephone call routing and delivery were changing, and the regulatory environment was nearing a historic shake up. That began in 1974, when U.S. Attorney General William B. Saxbe filed an antitrust lawsuit against the American Telephone & Telegraph Company (AT&T).

History has all but forgotten Saxbe, but the public service of our 70th attorney general deserves remembrance. A lawyer and World War Two bomber pilot, Saxbe was a U.S. senator from Ohio when the Watergate Scandal engulfed the Nixon administration after the 1972 election. Following the 'Saturday Night Massacre' (in which both Attorney General Elliott Richardson and Deputy Attorney General William Ruckelshaus abruptly resigned), Solicitor General Robert H. Bork accepted an interim appointment as Acting Attorney General. Saxbe, considered by President Nixon to be a safe choice to replace Richardson and Bork, was sworn in on January 4, 1974.

Senator William B. Saxbe (OH)
credit. U.S. Senate Historical Office

William B. Saxbe (1916-2010) was a United States senator from Ohio when President Richard M. Nixon appointed him to be the nation's 70th attorney general. Saxbe initiated the landmark AT&T lawsuit without consulting the White House. Source: United States Senate Historical Office.

As the new attorney general, Saxbe was wary of the president's preoccupation with the Watergate Scandal. As a result, Saxbe had the Justice Department file the historic federal complaint against AT&T without even consulting the White House. The federal complaint alleged that AT&T and related parties acted together as an unlawful monopoly, using profits from the huge Western Electric subsidiary to subsidize its long distance network so as to stifle competition. Saxbe resigned as attorney general in February 1975, early in the Ford administration, but the antitrust case was unstoppable. The suit plodded along, originally being assigned to U.S. District Judge Joseph Waddy, but was eventually removed from his docket due to the judge's battle with cancer.

In 1978, the historic lawsuit was placed on the docket of U.S. District Judge Harold H. Greene, who received the matter during his first day on the federal bench. Greene grew impatient with the plodding nature of the case and, on January 15, 1981, he finally set a trial date. Roughly a year later, but only after a lengthy trial had almost been completed, the Justice Department and the defendants reached a settlement agreement. Judge Greene rejected initial settlement efforts but, on August 5, 1983, he finally approved a consent decree that would breakup the AT&T long distance telephone monopoly. Beginning in 1984 the decree would take effect, and the Bell Telephone System would be no more.

The voluminous case that garnered national attention dealt with more than the intricacies of antitrust law; it also considered technology. In particular, the last segment of infrastructure over which telephone calls were routed was considered "essential facilities." There, in what is called the local loop, the cost of the trunk and switching infrastructure was prohibitively high, which precluded any real competition. The legal remedy, contained within the consent degree, was to require access to those "essential facilities" by the Regional Bell Operating Companies (RBOCs). Of course, technology changes, and so too does the regulatory environment. A dozen years later, the Telecommunications Act of 1996 superseded the consent decree, and the first phase of the regulatory revolution was over.

After escaping from Nazi Germany Harold H. Greene (1923-2000) served in the U.S. Army intelligence service (left), where he interrogated enemy prisoners. After graduating from George Washington University Law School in 1952, Greene served as an assistant United States attorney and helped draft both the Civil Rights Act of 1964 and the Voting Rights Act of 1965. Appointed to the federal bench by President Jimmy Carter, Judge Greene quickly gained national attention for his deft handling of the AT&T case. The circa 1995 image (right) was taken later in his career. Images are courtesy of the Greene family and the Historical Society of the D.C. Circuit.

Along with changes in the regulatory landscape, the Quiet Revolution of SS7 was affected by technological changes that preceded Judge Greene's important rulings. Of particular interest are the technological changes that affected telephony outside of the local loop near a call's destination. One of those major advances involved communication satellites, and what we can refer to as a satcom revolution.[2] before satellites and transponder technology entered the picture, long distance calling on terrestrial telephone systems was often expensive and cumbersome. Satellites became a reality on October 5, 1957 when the Soviet Union launched *Sputnik 1*. *Sputnik* was a rudimentary design, but when it was launched into a low elliptical orbit it precipitated the Space Race and, in very short order, America's manned space program.

The first American satellite was Explorer 1, which was launched on January 31, 1958 by a Chrysler-built Juno I, a four-stage version of the U.S. Army's Redstone rocket.[3] *Explorer 1* was a scientific satellite; it was launched during the International Geophysical Year, but it also accomplished the political goal of catching up with the Soviet Union's space program. The first demonstration of a broadcast from outer space occurred during Project SCORE, an acronym for Space Communications by Orbiting Relay Equipment. The satellite was also named *SCORE*, and it was crude; *SCORE* was merely the shell of the Atlas-B launch vehicle. On December 18, 1958, it broadcast a message by President Dwight D. Eisenhower over the short wave radio band. Millions heard the president's words:

> *This is the President of the United States speaking. Through the*
> *marvels of scientific advance, my voice is coming to you via*
> *a satellite circling in outer space. My message is a simple one:*
> *Through this unique means I convey to you and all mankind,*
> *America's wish for peace on Earth and goodwill toward men*
> *everywhere.*[4]

So *SCORE*, as primitive as its design was, ushered in the new era of communications satellites.

The next major developments came during 1960, when three significant milestones were achieved. On April 1, 1960, *TIROS I* (Television Infrared Observation Satellite) was launched into a low, circular orbit.[5] *TIROS I* remained aloft for just 78 days, but the

17

televised weather images that it sent back to earth were significant. On August 12th, a balloon satellite named *Echo 1* was launched using a Thor-Delta launch vehicle. When the Mylar® skinned satellite was inflated in space, the satellite formed a 100-foot diameter sphere that was used as a passive reflector of telephone, radio and television signals.[6] Then, on October 4th, *Courier 1B* was launched into a low earth orbit.

TIROS (left) shown during prelaunch preparation, was America's first meteorological satellite. Image G-65-5216 from NASA GRIN database GPN-2002-000116. Source: NASA. Delta rocket (right) with an improved TIROS satellite (ITOS-B) that was lost after a launch on October 21, 1971 from NASA's Western Test Range in California. Source: NASA GRIN database number GPN-2000-001340.

Unlike the passive *Echo 1*, *Courier 1B* was the first satellite that could perform as a active repeater. On its second orbit, *Courier 1B* relayed a communication from President Eisenhower to the United Nations. The uplink was established from a U.S. Army Signal Corps facility in Ocean Township, New Jersey; the ground relay station was located in Puerto Rico. *Courier 1B* failed during orbit 228 after just 17 days but, despite its short operational life, it accomplished its mission goals.[7]

By 1961, Project Mercury and America's manned space program started to dominate public attention, but in the background improved launch vehicles, transponders and communication satellites were developed. On December 13, 1962, the *Relay 1* satellite was launched from Cape Canaveral by a Delta B launch vehicle and, shortly thereafter, achieved geosynchronous orbit. Aside from gathering scientific data on radiation, *Relay 1* made history, but with a tragic twist. On November 22, 1963, the satellite was to perform the first satellite relay of a television broadcast from the United States to Japan. The plan was to send a pre-recorded televised broadcast of an address by President John F, Kennedy, who was visiting Dallas, Texas that day. Instead, the first satellite relay of a television broadcast was of a hastily made program entitled *Record, Life of the late John F. Kennedy*. The program sparked by the tragic events of that day was seen simultaneously in the United States and Japan.

In August 1964, *Relay 1* again made history when it began to relay television broadcasts of the 1964 Summer Olympics. In fact, *Relay 1* served as the link between the United States and Europe. It operated in tandem with another satellite, *Syncom 3*, which handle the trans-Pacific link to *Relay 1*.[8]

Communication satellite technology continued to develop, although it was surpassed by the manned space program. *Syncom 3*, which was launched on August 19, 1964, was the first satellite that achieved a true geostationary orbit. Satellites in geostationary orbit are typically parked roughly 22,300 miles over the Equator. Satellite parking locations are established at 2-degree longitude increments, although multiple satellites can occupy a given station. *Syncom-3* was parked above the Equator at the International Date Line (i.e., 180 degrees east longitude), where it was perfectly located for duties as a Pacific Ocean relay. But as impressive as *Syncom 3* was, its capabilities were limited. *Syncom-3* had just two 2-watt transponders, and only one was a broadband unit to provide the necessary spectrum for television.[9]

In 1965, an international consortium named Intelsat launched *Intelsat I*, also known as the *Early Bird*, and parked it over the Equator at 28 degrees west longitude. The *Early Bird* sat over the Atlantic Ocean, more than 600 miles off the coast of Brazil, and became the first satellite in geostationary orbit over the Atlantic.[10] Although limited to one television channel (or 240 voice channels), *Early Bird* was just a beginning. The Intelsat II series included four satellites (*Intelsat II F1* through *Intelsat II F4*) with greatly expanded transponder capabilities, and Intelsat III (five satellites in service) even more so. But the Intelsat series spacecraft had a short service life and that, plus their available communications channels, made them unsuitable for telecommunications services over North America.[11] Fortunately, as Intelsat III spacecraft entered service, other factors continued to push the advance of satellite technologies.

By the late-1970s, the Satcom Revolution was nearly complete, with three companies (Western Union, AT&T and RCA) dominating the North American market. The technology had improved, and the spacecraft proved it. By the end of 1975 RCA Americom (as it was then called) was operating its *Satcom 1* satellite. Basically an RCA Astro-Electronics Division AS-1000 satellite, the spacecraft would be stabilized around all axes (i.e., antenna always pointed towards earth) and be equipped with 24 communications channels. Each channel could service 972 telephone circuits, or a color television signal.[12] *Satcom 1* was historic. The satellite was used to broadcast television signals for the major networks, although AT&T's terrestrial infrastructure continued in areas that lacked earth stations for downlinks into local markets. After the AT&T break up in 1984, the networks used only satellite links, enjoying tremendous reliability and lower costs as well. *Satcom 1* was also instrumental in the startup of many networks, such as ESPN, the Weather Channel and CNN.[13] Much had been accomplished since *Relay 1*, and much more would follow.

Of course most Americans are familiar with the Cellular Revolution. By 2011, there were an estimated 311 million wireless subscriber connections in the United States. That revolution could be roughly dated to 1996, at the time that the Telecommunications Act of 1996 became law. While many households have both wireline and cellular service, an increasing number eschew the traditional wired telephone connection altogether. But while the cellular revolution in telecommunications is quite familiar, the Quiet Revolution has gone almost completely unnoticed. Yet the difference between telephony of the past and present is stark.

Before cellphones became ubiquitous, voice communications relied on the old fashioned household telephone. With Plain Old Telephone Service (POTS), if any phone in a household was left uncradled, incoming calls could not be completed to that residential number. Worse yet, if the outside caller didn't hang up, the receiving party's house phone would then be unusable. Of course, there were no text or picture messages. And before the mid-1990s, the World Wide Web did not exist. Phone service was a lot more expensive. And direct dialing to India, France or the Philippines? No, there were special overseas operators for that. How quickly we forget!

At the end of the 2011 fall semester, college students faced pressures similar to those by an earlier generation in 1971. Completion of lab reports, course projects and prep for final exams were still time consuming and sometimes stressful events. But on campuses around the country, classmates and friends largely communicated with cellphones, text and email messages, and through social networks. They were able to stay in touch, communicating from their dorm, library or student center, or as a passenger in a friend's car. A cellphone call from Worcester, Massachusetts to Pasadena, California could be dialed directly, and without expensive toll charges. Students could text a parent if they were coming home for the weekend, running late due to traffic, or bringing along an unexpected friend. A son could call his father if he needed money for a date and, a few hours later, use caller ID to not answer his dad when ensconced in more pressing social matters.

Advances in technology can change society, and we are aware of these changes when they affect our own lives. New jet airliners make travel between distant continents not just possible, but routine. CAT scans, organ transplants and new medicines save and extend lives. Online college courses provide parents and working adults with greater access to higher education and, in some cases, their only access. And new social media enables distant friends to stay in touch. Yet almost completely unknown is the revolution in telephony that for roughly four decades has completely changed virtually everyone's life. Today, still operating outside of the general public's view, the final phase of that Quiet Revolution continues.

Prologue Footnotes

1 See 552 F. Supp. 131 (1982).

2 The term Satcom is used in a generic sense, referring to all satellite communication systems, as opposed to the formal name of the RCA Satcom series of satellites.

3 The Redstone is most familiar to the public as the launch vehicle for Project Mercury Astronaut Alan B. Shepard, Jr. and

his *Freedom 7* capsule, and Astronaut Virgil I. "Gus" Grissom and his *Liberty Bell 7* capsule.

4 Source: See *SCORE (Signal Communications by Orbiting Relay Equipment)*, GlobalSecurity.org, Sept. 20, 2006.

5 Referred to as either *TIROS-1* or *TIROS I* (using Roman numeral script). It was the first weather satellite, and was launched by a standard Thor-Able from Cape Canaveral, FL. Source: NASA.

6 Project Echo involved ground tests whereby the satellite was fully inflated inside a U.S. Navy blimp hangar in Weeksville, NC. The experimental satellite was built by the G. T. Schjeldahl Company in Northfield, MN. *Echo 1* was designed to be a passive reflector of microwave signals while operating in low Earth orbit. Source: NASA.

7 Note: The uplink was controlled by the U.S. Army Signal Corps in Fort Monmouth, NJ. The Earth station was located off base at what was then called the Deal Test Site. *Courier 1A* was lost in a post-launch failure during ascent, but *Courier 1B* was successful. *Courier 1A/B* were manufactured by the Western Development Labs (WDL) division of Philco, which is now the Space Systems/Loral division of Loral Space & Communications, Inc. Source(s): NASA and U.S. Army.

8 Source: NASA.

9 Source(s): NASA. See also *Birds In Hand: RCA and a Communication Revolution*, by Archie T. Miller (Kindle Edition). Author's Note: Lines of longitude extend between the geographic North Pole and the geographic South Pole of the Earth. 0 degrees longitude extends through the Royal Observatory in Greenwich, England, and is referred to as the Prime Meridian. Lines of longitude that lie east of Cambridge, England increase in numeric value and are considered "east longitudes." The International dateline, at 180 degrees east longitude, is where the date changes, with east longitude time zones being ahead of the west longitude time zones. Lines of longitude that lie west of the Prime Meridian are not given negative values, but are denoted by the prefix W(est), in the same manner that easterly longitudes have the prefix E(ast).

10 Ibid.

11 Ibid.

12 Ibid.

13 Author's Note: CNN was scheduled to use RCA's *Satcom 3*, which was destroyed during a post-launch explosion on December 12, 1979. However, CNN's service inauguration date of June 1, 1980 was achieved when RCA temporarily made available transponders on another satellite.

Section One

Setting the Stage: Evolution of the Underlying Technologies

To the President of the United States, Washington,
...The Queen is convinced that the President will join with her fervently hoping that the electric cable which now connects Great Britain with the United States will prove an additional link between the nations, whose friendship is founded upon their common interest and reciprocal esteem.

- Excerpt of the trans-Atlantic telegraph message from Her Majesty Queen Victoria to U.S. President James Buchanan, on August 16, 1858.

To Her Majesty Victoria, The Queen of Great Britain,
The President cordially reciprocates the congratulations of her Majesty the Queen, on the success of the great international enterprise accomplished by the science, skill and indomitable energy of the two countries. It is a triumph more glorious, because far more useful to mankind, than was ever won by conqueror on the field of battle.

- From the reply message of President James Buchannan to Queen Victoria of England, referring to her trans-Atlantic telegram.

Like the revolution in telephony that would begin a century and a half later, 1825 was a relatively quiet year. In the United States, John Quincy Adams was elected president, not by the Electoral College, but by the House of Representatives. That unusual event occurred on February 9th; it came about because none of the four candidates in the 1824 election reccived enough electoral votes to win.[1] Eight months later, on October 26, another quiet but important event occurred when the Erie Canal opened in upstate New York.

Extending from Buffalo (at the eastern end of Lake Erie) to Albany, the 363-mile trip could be made on a comfortable, mule-drawn barge in just ten days. Despite their shallow draft, the canal boats could carry grain, beef, lumber and machinery until winter weather interrupted the service. For passengers, canal boats were more comfortable and convenient than traveling by horseback or stagecoach. And most importantly, for the first time there was a practical transportation route that linked New York City, at the mouth of the Hudson River, with Lake Erie and the nation's Midwest. Not bad at all for an era that preceded steam locomotives and railways.

Across the Atlantic, London, England surpassed Beijing, China (traditionally spelled Peking) as the largest city in the world. The Stockton and Darlington Railway, the world's first modern railway, commenced service in the northeast part of England; it began with one of the earliest examples of a steam engine. Meanwhile, a bad loan that involved the Bank of England and dozens of other banks led to the Panic of 1825.[2] But a financial collapse was averted, thanks to a rescue loan by Banque de France in Paris. King George IV still reigned over the British Empire that year, while Charles X was King of France. Farther east, Alexander I was near the end of his reign as both Emperor of Russia and King of Poland. In South America, Simón Bolívar relinquished his title of 'Dictator' of Peru, choosing instead to be called the 'Liberator.' Perhaps there would be cause for optimism.

1825 was also in an age of technological change. It was within the period called the Industrial Revolution, when waterpower started to drive textile machinery, and machines of all sorts began to replace human and animal power. The steam engine was still in its infancy and, despite the Industrial Revolution, traveling at sea had advanced only as far as the clipper ship. 1825 was still within of the Age of Sail, a time when homes and businesses operated without electricity, and when the telegraph had yet to arrive. Letters of other messages were delivered over land by horseback, stagecoach or horse-drawn wagon, and across oceans by large windjammers. But that was about to change. Just as steam locomotives were starting to appear, the civilized world was developing practical experience with electricity and simple electrical devices. Early forms of telecommunications would follow.

The fundamental mechanism that permitted the coming advances in telecommunications was the electromagnet, developed by the Englishman William Sturgeon in 1825.[3] Five years later, the American inventor Joseph Henry went a step further. Henry connected a mile long cable to a remote electromagnetic device. When the cable was energized it activated the distant electromagnet, which caused a mechanical movement that in turn rang a bell. Henry had demonstrated that communicating by signal over a distance was possible, but it was only a precursor.[4] The next advance would occur in Russia. Between 1832-34, the world's first electromagnetic telegraph system was created and tested in St. Petersburg (known as Leningrad from 1924-1991) by the diplomat and inventor Pavel Shilling.[5] Shilling's prototype system was an important step in developing telegraph technology, but the device's short range made it impractical. The next major steps occurred in England.

In 1836, William Fothergill Cooke wanted to take Schilling's methodology a little farther. Cooke's efforts were helped when he was introduced to the eminent electrical engineer Charles Wheatstone. (The introduction was made by Peter Roget, who would himself become famous for producing the first thesaurus.) It was a fortuitous meeting. In 1834 Wheatstone had received an appointment as a professor of experimental physics at King's College. Shortly thereafter, he became prominent for his experiments to determine the velocity of electricity within a closed circuit. Two years later, at about the time that he was introduced to Cooke, Wheatstone became a fellow of the Royal Society. Working together, Cooke and Wheatstone developed an electromagnetic telegraph that was first tested on a railroad line between Euston and Camden.[6] In May, 1837 Cooke and Wheatstone received a United Kingdom patent for what was their first practical telegraph, and in 1839 the two began a commercial service along a thirteen-mile stretch of railway lines.[7]

Other advances followed. In 1846, Werner von Siemens added make-or-break contacts; this led to his "pointer" telegraph, thereby increasing its practicality.[8] Back in America, an artist named Samuel F. B. Morse developed his own telegraph system. Yet Morse, who relied on prior advances, was not the inventor of the telegraph, and he did not work alone. Faced with the problem of sending a signal any appreciable distance, Morse received a solution from Professor Leonard Gale, who taught chemistry at New York University. To provide an adequate signal over extended distances, Gale recommended the use of relays within the telegraph circuit. The relays functioned as a form of digital amplifier, and were an integral part of Morse's 1838 patent application. Morse also improved the technology by incorporating a double wire. On June 20, 1842 the U.S. Patent Office awarded Morse Patent Number 1,647 for "Improvement In The Mode Of Communicating Information By Signals By The Application Of Electro-Magnetism." So Morse, contrary to some of his protestations, did not invent the telegraph, but he certainly improved it.[9]

By the middle of the nineteenth century, much of Europe (but not the United Kingdom) began using Morse's technology. The International Morse Code, which was largely developed by Morse's assistant Alfred Vail, also came into widespread use.[10] But as telegraph service spread between distant cities and across borders, the barrier of channels, gulfs and oceans remained. What moved things along were the more or less concurrent advances of Victorian-era science and technology. In particular, knowledge of the basic elements of nature expanded, while fundamental principles of thermodynamics, and the relationship between electricity and magnetism were revealed.

In 1850, Rudolf Clausius put forth a statement of the first and second laws of thermodynamics.[11] Four years later, William Rankine (famous for the Rankine cycle) introduced a concept of thermodynamics that is now known as entropy.[12] And in the early 1860s, James Clerk Maxwell was developing foundations for the famous equations that would one day bear his name; they denote fundamental relationships of electromagnetism.[13] Advances in science and technology would affect the capabilities signaling apparatus, and the then yet to be named practices of telecommunications.

So by the mid-nineteenth century, the stage was then set for the laying of underwater telegraph cables. The first significant underwater cable was laid under the English Channel during 1850, but it was poorly built and had to be replaced the following year.[14] Then, in 1853, submarine telegraph cables were laid between Ireland and Scotland, London and Paris and from England to the Netherlands.[15] [16] [17] The next major challenge would be a trans-Atlantic cable, and with that the difficulties would rise exponentially. That effort began in 1858, two years before the American Civil War began.

The 1858 cable started from Valentia Island, off the western coast of Ireland, ran across the seabed of the Atlantic Ocean and came ashore at Trinity Bay on the northeast coast of Newfoundland. The cable validated the concept of trans-Atlantic telegrams, but transmission rates were extremely slow. In fact, it would take hours to send even short messages using International Morse Code. In any event, the cable lasted only twenty three days of service.[18] But in 1866, the large ship *Great Eastern* successfully laid another trans-Atlantic cable, and this one was successful.[19] William Thomson, the eminent physicist who acted as the consulting engineer, was knighted for his work on the cable.

Thomson is best known to science students as Lord Kelvin, for whom the Kelvin temperature scale is named.[20] Yet perhaps the most important scientist was the little known Oliver Heaviside, a brilliant recluse who independently studied issues affecting the propagation of signals along submarine cables. Heaviside's brilliance was established when he evaluated the undersea signaling to Denmark, correctly identifying the two main technical issues as being the resistance and leakage of the cable. Heaviside's solution of using loading coils would have profound implications in long-distance telephony, but his views were often ignored (even by Lord Kelvin).[21]

The S.S. Great Eastern, photographed in Milford Haven, Wales, circa 1870. The 692-long sailing steamship had an iron hull, and was the world's largest ocean going vessel in its time. Four steam engines drove side paddles and a propeller,

28

Ten years later, another great stride was made in telecommunications. The Canadian Alexander Graham Bell, who began experimenting with electrical voice transmissions in 1865 while living in London, England, further refined his technology in America. After a few years teaching deaf students to speak, Bell resumed experiments with the propagation of sound using a harmonic telegraph, an apparatus that produced different tones and which was connected to a wire electric circuit. Many other inventors also pursued experiments, notably Thomas A. Edison (telegraph improvements),[22] Charles Grafton Page (experiments with "galvanic music"),[23] French experimenter Charles Bourseul (digital tone experiments),[24] Danish inventor Poul la Cour (audio telegraphs),[25] German inventor Johann Philipp Reis (the Reis telephone, with a make-or-break circuit)[26] and the Italian-American inventor Antonio Meucci (sound telegraphs).[27]

Alexander Graham Bell (1847-1922) was awarded United States Patent No. 174,465. Image of Alexander Graham Bell is in the public domain, PD-US. Retrieved on December 8, 2012 from: http://upload.wikimedia.org/wikipedia/commons/thumb/1/10/Alexander _Graham_Bell.jpg/461px-Alexander_Graham_Bell.jpg.

Some of the above inventors preceded Bell with certain developments in telephony, but Bell was not deterred. Working with the aid of Thomas A. Watson, Bell was able to successfully transmit voice over short distances with an electromagnetic apparatus that has been referred to as a "gallows phone." Bell's attorney filed a patent application on February 14, 1876. But the story did not end there.

On the same day (and perhaps earlier), Elisha Gray filed his own patent caveat (i.e., a preliminary application) with the U.S. Patent Office. Gray was the better engineer, and had previously been awarded a patent for an "Electric Telegraph for Transmitting Musical Tones." A dispute over which applicant was the rightful inventor ensued, a matter that remains controversial to this day. However, after Bell completed additional tests (themselves controversial), he was awarded U.S. Patent Number 174,465 on March 7, 1876. Gray continued inventing, and received U.S. Patent Number 386,815 on July 31, 1888 for his "Telautograph," a precursor to the ubiquitous fax machine. Alexander Graham Bell went on to create the telephone company that bore his name, and also became an early developer of aircraft.[28] Unfortunately, the inventor relied on borrowed money to fund his activities, and relinquished any interest in the companies that used his name. As a result, Bell remained a man of very modest means despite his universal fame.

Elisha Gray (1835-1901) was regarded by many as the true inventor of a practical telephone, but the U.S. patent was awarded to Alexander Graham Bell. Gray went on to invent a device called the telautograph in 1887, for which he was awarded U.S. Patent No. 386,815. The telautograph was a precursor to the modern facsimile device. Courtesy of the Oberlin College Archives.

Telephone service began to proliferate during the 1890s. This development was more or less concurrent with the electrification of cities (with alternating current) and the appearance of automobiles. By that time, Alexander Graham Bell was retired from the telephone business. The American Telephone & Telegraph Company, or AT&T, was formed in 1885; it would be the long distance carrier for what was called the American Bell Telephone Company. However, this was the end of the gaslight era, and most Americans did not have a telephone, an automobile or electricity. Much of the growth in telephones occurred after World War One ended and, at least for many businesses, telephone service competed with telegraph companies for long distance communications.

Much attention has been directed to Alexander Graham Bell, Elisha Gray and other telephone inventors, but very little has gone to Tivadar Puskás. Puskás was a Hungarian inventor, collaborator of Thomas A. Edison, and the person credited with inventing the telephone exchange.[29] George W. Coy, another inventor, designed what is often referred to as the first telephone exchange that saw commercial use; it began service in New Haven, Connecticut in January, 1878.[30] Almon Brown Strowger is another forgotten inventor. It is Strowger who invented the so-called Strowger switch and, on March 10, 1891, he received U.S. Patent No. 447,918 Much attention has been directed to Alexander Graham Bell, Elisha Gray and other ('Automatic Telephone Exchange').

The Strowger switch was an electromechanical, step-by-step design; it was first used in LaPorte, Indiana on November 3, 1892.[31] Significantly, the system architecture permitted expansion so that, as the number of telephone subscribers grew, the switching capabilities could be scaled up. In fact, it was the Strowger switch that introduced busy signals to telephony. Still, Strowger's early mechanical design was cumbersome and, while it improved the star of the art, there were still significant limits to traffic. The step-by-step switch architecture also resulted in a very noisy apparatus, quite unlike modern switches. As a point of interest, telephone company technicians in the early decades of the twentieth century sometimes used the noise of the mechanical relays to troubleshoot connection errors in the switch. Strowger's design was refined in Europe before gaining much acceptance in America, and then only after 1938.

It is important to note here that while this mini-book is a story of technology, people are an important part of that story. Included among those people are the telephone operators. Early operators, circa 1880-1910, often made local connections based on names, rather than telephone numbers. Operators would also monitor call progress, sometimes listening in or, a little later, by monitoring an annunciator lamp. When the call was finished, if the caller did not have an additional call request, the operator would end the connection.

Before long, most local operators started using local numbers, or combinations of local subscriber names and numbers, when making connections. Three digit and four digit numbers were more than sufficient in most calling areas and, for calls outside of a local area, other operators would be involved. Color coded plugs were added to switchboards, and operators were able to immediately see if a subscriber's line was active, disconnected or if a number had been changed. Operators also had to have good general knowledge about how the system functioned beyond their switchboard office, as calls out of the area, special calls (e.g., collect calls) and system failures would all involve operator intervention.

Early telephones reflected the state of the emerging technology and, because they were so different from contemporary devices, they also deserve some attention. In the late nineteenth and early twentieth century, telephones were typically mounted inside a small cabinet, the latter usually being attached to a wall. A hand crank would protrude outside the cabinet, thereby allowing the caller to crank a magneto.

The telephone magneto, basically a mechanical signal generator, would produce anywhere from 1 to 5 amps of current and would signal an operator (or in some cases, a down line party) that you were making a call.[32] When the operator answered, the caller would identify the party to whom the call was being placed and the operator would make the connection. Because the arrival of telephones preceded the electrification of the United States, telephones often had hand cranks to rotate an internal magneto. The rotation of the magneto generated direct (d-c) current, which enabled an electrical signal to be sent to the local switchboard.[33] With twentieth century electrification came simpler phones that eliminated hand cranking, but until automation reached the switchboard even local calls were labor intensive.

Looking at the marketplace, the numbers tell the story of public acceptance, and demand, for telephone service. If one begins a trend line at 1881, it will show that the nation had roughly fifty thousand telephone subscribers. By 1900 the number of subscribers had increased to 600,000, and by 1905 it had increased almost fourfold, to 2.2 million.[34] Five years later, in 1910, the rate of increase was slightly lower, but was still almost three-fold – to 5.8 million.[35] Along with the impressive number gains came changes in the business and regulatory environment.

In 1907, AT&T acquired Western Union, and thereafter effectively monopolized both long distance telephone and telegraph service. But in 1913, AT&T agreed to divest itself of Western Union and provide long distance connections to small, independent phone exchanges.[36] By early 1915, the first cross-county trunk line was finished. The first transcontinental call was made on January 25th, when Alexander Graham Bell picked up a telephone receiver in a New York City office and called his former assistant Thomas A. Watson, who was waiting for the call in San Francisco.[37] It took five telephone operators 23 minutes to complete the connection.

The inauguration of cross-country telephone service was significant, but two big details should not be overlooked. First, the size of the lower 48 contiguous states would ensure that it would take many more years to complete the trunk lines and switch infrastructure that would link all major cities. The second big detail was World War One. The Great War, as it was then called, began in 1914 but America remained out of the conflict until April 1917. Effective telephone and telegraph communications were a national priority so, in June 1918, the federal government took control of AT&T's telephone system and gave jurisdiction to the U.S. Postal Service. Some might wonder if giving the Post Office control over AT&T was a good idea. Suffice it to say that by July 1919 (eight months after the war was over), the government relinquished control.[38] Not until 1934, when AT&T became a regulated monopoly under the authority of the Federal Communications Commission (FCC), would the company face significant federal constraints.

At this point, you should appreciate the salient points of scientific and technological development, beginning from the early nineteenth century and continuing through the first two decades of the twentieth century. We have not looked at all of these developments, but have covered enough to serve our immediate purposes. It should also be evident that telephony and telegraph service were sister technologies and had a great deal in common. In the next section, we will look at the continued development of switch technologies from roughly 1938 to the period shortly just before SS7 was born. Those were the Pre-Revolution years.

⟨⟩   Side Notes for Students, Teachers and Parents   ⟨⟩

The foregoing information is provided so that you will have a greater perspective of how ding our understanding of electrical and magnetic phenomena, occurred in the nineteenth modern technologies developed. You will note that major advances in physics, inclu and early twentieth century. The same is true for chemistry and various branches of mathematics.

Having some understanding of major developments in technology, and a general knowledge of the math and science principles upon which various technologies are based, can ease the journey through the K-12 education system, and beyond. In particular, having a year of chemistry and a year of physics in high school will provide a useful base of knowledge. These are rigorous courses, but I would be more impressed with a student who earned a 'C' in chemistry or physics than a student who earned a higher grade in a less rigorous science course.

In math, having a good understanding of algebra is important. Two other mathematical topics are extremely valuable: i.e., logarithms and trigonometry. Logarithms (or logs) deal with exponents; they are the inverse of an exponent. Do not be put off by the name, as the rules are straightforward. If you like to think of relationships, you will enjoy using logarithms in scientific applications. Trigonometry derives from geometry, and it too is all about relationships. In particular, trig (as it is called) provides a methodology for determining values for the sides of triangles. Using trig can be a useful and fascinating way to solve many science problems. It is something to look forward to, not something to fear or avoid.

Of course, not all readers of this text will want to be engineers or scientists. Some students will have interests in literature, the arts or social sciences. Yet in the twenty first century workplace, there will be an increased need for knowledge workers who possess strong interdisciplinary backgrounds. English and literature majors may find jobs writing training material for engineering departments, or end users of products. Sociologists may investigate the affects of a particular technology on a customer base, and musicians may collaborate with web page designers on interactive media. So we will all need some background in math, science and technology. It can be a wonderful journey.

Section One Footnotes

1 Note: The 1824 election had four candidates: Andrew Jackson, John Quincy Adams, William Harris Crawford and Henry Clay. None of the candidates received the required 131 electoral votes needed to win the election, which sent the election to the U.S. House of Representatives.

2 Note: seventy banks failed in England. For details of the macro-economy and condition of financial markets in England between the end of the Napoleonic Wars (1815) and the Panic, see 'Commentary' by Prof. Michael D. Bordo in the May/June edition of *Review*, published by the Federal Reserve Bank of St. Louis.

3 Note: Sturgeon's prototype apparatus used a bare copper that wire. His 1824 paper was submitted to the British Royal Society of Arts, Manufacturers and Commerce.

4 Note: Henry (1797-1878) discovered self-inductance and, independently of Michael Faraday, he discovered mutual inductance. The SI unit for inductance is the henry, named in honor of this inventor. See 'Joseph Henry' in the Distinguished Members Gallery, National Academy of Sciences (2005).

5 See 'Milestones: Schilling's Pioneering Telegraphy, 1828-1837' in IEEE Milestones (2009), IEEE Global History Network.

6 Note: Experiment of July 25, 1837 was conducted over a 1.5 mile distance along the London and North Western Railway. See *The Scientific Papers of Sir Charles Wheatstone, D.C.L. F.R.S.,* published by the Physical Society of London. Note also that Wheatstone is perhaps most well known for the Wheatstone bridge, which engineering students use to

determine the resistance of a conductor. However, the method was first developed by Samuel Hunter Christie of the Royal Military Academy. See 'The Genesis of the Wheatstone Bridge' by Stig Ekelof in the *Engineering Science and Education Journal*, Vol. 10, No. 1, February 1, 2001, pp 37-40.

7 Note: July 1939, between the Paddington and West Drayton stations of the Great Western railroad.

8 Note: The pointer would point to the letter that was being transmitted.

9 Ibid footnote 6. Credit for inventing the telegraph is shared by Sir William Fothergill Cooke (1806-1879) and Sir Charles Wheatstone, FRS (1802-1875). United Kingdom Patent application granted on June 12, 1837 and preceded the work of Samuel Morse in the United States.

10 Note: International Morse Code (aka Modern International Morse Code) was developed in Europe. It was first created in 1848 by Freidrich Clemens Gerke and, with some changes, was adapted in 1865 as the standard by the International Telegraphy Congress (in Paris). It subsequently became the standard of the International Telecommunications Union (ITU). The original American Morse Code (or Railroad Code), having been supplanted, fell out of use.

11 Note: The first law of thermodynamics states that the increase in [internal] energy of a system equals the heat applied to that system minus work done by the system: i.e., $U = Q - W$. The second law of thermodynamics defines entropy. In 1855, Clausius developed a mathematical expression for the second law that came to be known as the Clausius Theorem or, alternatively, as the Inequality of Clausius. It is used to explain the relationship between heat flow into or out of a system and entropy.

12 Note: Rankine, along with Rudolf Clausius and William Thomson (later known as Lord Kelvin), established thermodynamics as a distinct scientific discipline. Rankine and Clausius had slightly different views of entropy, and Clausius' view is accepted today. See 'On the Geometrical Representation of Expansive Energy of Heat, and the Theory

of Thermo-Dynamic Engines' by William J. M. Rankine (1854).

13 See *A Treatise on Electricity and Magnetism (Volumes 1 & 2)*, by James Clerk Maxwell (1873), and the predecessor paper *A Dynamic Theory of the Electromagnetic Field – 1865*, by James Clerk Maxwell (1865).

14 Note: The Anglo-French Telegraph Company used a copper cable that was coated with gutta-percha, but having no other insulation, August 1850.

15 Note: This cable ran from Donaghadee, Ireland to Portpatrick, Scotland.

16 Note: Linked by the Submarine Telegraph Company.

17 Note: The North Sea cable extended from Orford Ness to The Hague.

18 Note: The cable failed on September 18, 1858 after carrying 271 messages. The cause of that failure has most often been placed on the application of excessive voltage by the chief electrician, Edward Whitehouse.

19 Note: The S.S. *Great Eastern*, at 692-feet length overall, was the largest ship in the world when the cable was laid. Launched in 1858 on the River Thames in London, the ship was made of iron, and boasted a combination of sail and steam power. It was capable of carrying 4,000 passengers around the world without refueling.

20 Note: Sir William Thomson was knighted in 1866, and was elevated to the House of Lords in 1892. At that time he assumed the title Baron Kelvin, of Largs in the County of Ayr, and hence was known as Lord Kelvin. Thomson was the first scientist to serve in Britain's upper chamber.

21 Note: Heaviside was perhaps the most brilliant of the scientists who developed Maxwell's equations from their early forms. Heaviside also studied line losses in long distance telegraphy, and was instrumental in determining that [induction] loading coils could extend the transmission range of telegraph signals. See *The Maxwellians (Cornell History of Science)*, by Bruce J. Hunt (1994). See also *Oliver Heaviside:*

The Life, Work and Times of an Electrical Genius of the Victorian Age, by Paul J. Nahin.

22 Note: Edison's telegraph patents generally begin with Patent No. 91527, dated June 29, 1869, for 'Improvement In Printing Telegraphs' [also described as "Improvements in Electro-Magnetic Printing Telegraphs" with the patent description]. Altogether, Edison's telegraph and telephone patents numbered in the hundreds.

23 Note: Page used a double helix coil in his apparatus, which was basically a spiral conductor underneath a horseshoe magnet. The "galvanic music" was experienced when the current in the circuit was interrupted.

24 Note: Bourseul used "make or break" signaling, which was digital, in his audio experiments. Because Bourseul's signals could not emulate all of the analog sound wave effects (e.g., consonants), it was an intermediate step in the development of sound propagation, albeit an important one.

25 Note: La Cour used tuning forks to impose multiple signals on a single telegraph line, each message having its own discrete frequency. La Cour's effort to obtain a Unites States telephone patent were challenged, with Alexander Graham Bell prevailing in 1876. But la Cour did create a "phonic wheel" – basically, a synchronous motor that was excited by a tuning fork – for which he received a patent in 1877. The phonic wheel was important for its uses in multiplex telegraphy.

26 Note: Reis produced prototype telephones, but his work did not significantly advance the technology.

27 Note: Meucci developed what this author will refer to as precursors to the telephone. The significance of his work was, and is, controversial.

28 Note: The Bell Telephone Company was incorporated on July 9, 1877 by Gardiner come to be known as National Bell Telephone morphed into the American Bell Telephone Company as a result of mergers. On March 3, 1885, the American Telephone and Telegraph Company (the original

AT&T) was incorporated. Bell himself was never a major shareholder in any of the companies that bore his name.

In aviation, Bell collaborated with Samuel Pierpont Langley (then head of the Smithsonian Institute) on early flight experiments, circa 1896-1903. Langley's unmanned *Aerodrome* was the first heavier-than-air aircraft to successfully achieve powered flight (in 1896). Bell later co-founded the Aerial Experiment Association (AEA), on Sept. 30, 1907. This group, a Canadian-American research organization, built and successfully flew five different early aircraft before it disbanded on March 31, 1909. One of the collaborators was Glenn H. Curtiss, a famous American designer and manufacturer of aircraft. His fourth aircraft, *Silver Dart* (also called *Aerodrome No. 4*), became the first aircraft to fly in Canada on February 23, 1909.

29 Note: Puskás was working for Thomas A. Edison in 1877 when he developed the exchange. Puskás later handled Edison's European affairs.

30 Note: George W. Coy's telephone exchange was part of the District Telephone Company of New Haven, which was incorporated on January 15, 1878. The central office switchboard was located in a storefront in the Boardman Building, which was at the corner of State and Chapel Streets, New Haven, Connecticut (demolished in 1973). Coy, who was licensed to use Bell technology, had just twenty-one subscribers who paid $1.50/month for their telephone service when he started. Coy's switchboard accommodated eight party lines, each of which could handle a dozen customers. The company morphed into what became known as the Southern New England Telephone Company in 1882. Source: National Park Service, National Historical Landmarks Program, Withdrawal of National Historic Landmark Designation: Site of the First Telephone Exchange (prior to demolition). See also *Race on the Line: Gender, Labor and Technology in the Bell System*, 1880-1980, by Venus Green, p. 20.

31 Note: The exchange was part of the Strowger Automatic Telephone Company, which had approximately 75 subscribers. La Porte, Indiana was Strowger's hometown at the time.

32 Source: telephonymuseum.com

33 Note: The electrification of the United States required generating stations that could produce large quantities of alternating current, along with substation transformers and transmission lines. Although Thomas A. Edison favored direct current, advocates of alternating current (mainly George Westinghouse and Nikola Tesla) proved that Edison was wrong. The first major generating facility was the Edward Dean Adams Station at Niagara Falls, New York. The Dean Adams Station began operations on August 25, 1895 using Westinghouse generators; supplied electricity to Buffalo and Niagara Falls, New York. See 'Milestones: Adams Hydroelectric Generating Plant, 1895' at the IEEE Global History Network. See also *Empire of Light: Edison, Tesla, Westinghouse, and the Race to Electrify the World*, by Jill Jonnes (2004).

34 Source: AT&T Archives.

35 Ibid.

36 Ibid.

37 Source: http://www.corp.att.com/attlabs/reputation/timeline/15tel.html

38 See Proclamation of the President [Woodrow Wilson], 40 stat. 1807, issued July 22, 1918, effective August 1, 1918. See also U.S. Post Office report, 1921: *Government Control and Operation of Telegraph, Telephone and Marine Cable Systems, August 1, 1918 to July 31, 1919*. Source: Government Printing Office.

Section Two

The Pre-Revolution Years

Without him, none of the things we know today would exist. The whole digital revolution started with him.

> – Dr. Neil J. A. Sloane, AT&T Fellow, recipient of the Chauvenet Prize of the Mathematical Association of America (1979), on his Bell Laboratory colleague Claude Shannon.

The Strowger switch, and other step-by-step devices, provided a major improvement in the call routing process. Yet it was only an incremental step in the advance of telephony. After World War One, customer direct dialing on rotary telephones reduced the need for human intervention on most calls. Yet the Bell Telephone System remained heavily dependent on operators, both at local exchanges and in the connection of long distance toll calls. Effective call handling and routing was essential, if for no other reason that the number of phone calls being made was growing exponentially.

There were also economic imperatives in telephony. For one thing, the very large numbers of operators and technicians that were needed created a heavy economic burden. The costs associated with that labor, the telephone network infrastructure, research, engineering and administrative costs could only be paid for if sufficient service revenue were obtained. Meanwhile, managers had to plan and implement a larger and improved system. Even in the early part of the twentieth century, mathematical modeling played an important role. Not all of the research occurred in the United States.

Building A Theoretical Base for Telephony

One of the early researchers who played a significant role in improving telephony was Agner K. Erlang (1878-1929), an electrical engineer and mathematician. Erlang worked for the Copenhagen Telephone Company (CTC) from 1908 until just before his death.

Most significantly, Erlang pioneered queuing theory and it's applications to traffic engineering. In 1909, Erlang published 'The Theory of Probabilities and Telephone Conversations,' an important work that established that random telephone calls were represented by a Poisson distribution. Then, in 1917, he published another seminal paper, this one entitled 'Solution of Some Problems in the Theory of Probabilities of Significance in Automatic Telephone Exchanges.' In his 1917 paper, Erlang presented what would become his famous and extremely useful formula, $E = \lambda h$ in which the traffic offered to a system, E, equals the product of the call arrival rate, λ, times the average call holding time, h.

Both the American Bell Telephone System and the British Post Office (which operated Great Britain's telephone system) carefully studied Erlang's works. However, Erlang's 1917 paper was written during World War One, and the immediate needs of the war effort pre-empted many additional studies. Yet it was clear early on that probability and queuing theory would play significant roles in telephone traffic management and system design.

One of Erlang's most important revelations was that a Poisson process (i.e., in probability theory, a stochastic process) could be used to model a system of incoming calls to a telephone switchboard/switch. Bear in mind that in a stochastic (i.e., random) process a finite number of random variables in a system are evaluated over a time interval. Poisson processes are continuous time processes. (More on this will be found in the sidebar notes at the end of the chapter.) But as important as Erlang's work was, it didn't improve the technology of the telephone system itself.

Then in 1906, just a couple of years before Agner Erlang went to work at the Copenhagen Telephone Company, a New York City-based electrical engineer named Lee de Forest developed a diode vacuum tube. The following year, de Forest went a step further by adding a third electrode between the vacuum tube's filament (i.e., the cathode) and the plate-shaped anode. The resulting tube was called the triode Audion, and it proved to be an extremely effective amplifier of signals. In fact, it was the electronic amplification that was pioneered by de Forest's triode Audion that enabled future transcontinental telephone calls. Prior to effective amplification, even the very useful loading circuits could not maintain a telephone transmission across the entire country. So the triode would be crucial to electronic circuits until the transistor was invented in 1947. De Forest's advances in electronics established that telephony would derive from multiple math and science disciplines, and that trend would also involve early computers.

In 1936, two years before the crossbar switches began to appear in the Bell Telephone System, twenty year old Claude E. Shannon arrived in Cambridge, Massachusetts. A recent graduate of the University of Michigan, Shannon began working on graduate degrees in mathematics and electrical engineering at the Massachusetts Institute of Technology (MIT). MIT provided enormous opportunities, one of which was the chance to work with university vice-president Vannevar Bush's differential analyzer.

Vannevar Bush (1890-1974), one of the great engineers of the twentieth century, was dean of the engineering school at the Massachusetts Institute of Technology when Claude Shannon arrived as a graduate student. Bush was prominent because of his work on analog computers and the design of digital circuits. During World War Two Bush was an initiator of the Manhattan Project, in addition to being President Franklin D. Roosevelt's chief science advisor. Public domain image, PD-US. Source: U.S. Office of Emergency Management. Retrieved on December 8, 2012 from: http://upload.wikimedia.org/wikipedia/commons/archive/e/ea/201204 22134806%21Vannevar_Bush_portrait.jpg.

The differential analyzer was an early analog computer, and it operated mechanically. In order to solve differential equations by integration, the differential analyzer used a family of wheels and mechanical discs. Bush developed his computer between 1928-31 with the help of Harold Loch Hazen, and derivative machines were soon built in England and Norway. Having six mechanical integrators gave Bush's computer the capacity to solve fairly advanced problems, and it was the first such analog device to become popular in America's scientific community. Shannon, with undergraduate degrees in both mathematics and electrical engineering, was hired as a research assistant to work with the early computer.

In working with the differential analyzer, Shannon became fascinated with the methodology. Each of the integrators was a gear mechanism, capable of operating at variable speeds and operating in tandem with a torque amplifier. The torque amplifier functioned much like a flywheel on an automotive drivetrain; it would increase the torque of an output shaft that would always match the speed of the input shaft. Bush originally referred to his design as a continuous integraph, but he later adapted the differential analyzer nomenclature.

As an engineer, Shannon's fascination with the mechanical computer is understandable. But Shannon was also a mathematician, and as he looked at the movements of the machine he saw a nexus to mathematics. In particular, his thoughts returned to a familiar topic: i.e., Boolean algebra.

As an undergraduate at the University of Michigan, Shannon studied the mathematical logic that was developed by George Boole almost a century earlier. Some side notes about Boolean algebra (or Boolean logic) are provided at the end of this section. Suffice it to say that Boolean algebra is a binary algebra; it uses just two values in the domain (0,1). As you will see in the side notes, Boolean logic can be used to produce truth tables along with algebraic solutions to problems. It is not surprising that as he worked with the differential analyzer, Shannon thought that by using Boolean algebra he could develop a faster and better system.[1] Looking a step further to engineering applications, he could foresee a method for simplifying the operation of telephone system switches. Shannon delved into this and, in partial fulfillment of the requirements for his master's degree, he produced a thesis entitled 'A Symbolic Analysis of Relay and Switching Circuits.' The thesis was presented in 1938 at about the same time that the 1XB crossbar switch came into use; it was published by the Massachusetts Institute of Technology in 1940.[2]

Dr. Claude Shannon, pictured at a maze, was the researcher whose pioneering work on communication theory led to the Information Age. Courtesy of AT&T Archives and History Center.

Claude Shannon was not the only one to take this approach. In 1935, the Russian scientist and engineer Victor Shestakov proposed his own theory about a system of electric switches that was based on Boolean algebra. However, Shestakov's paper was not published until 1941, and by that summer Russia and Germany were engaged in massive land battles within Soviet territory. Shannon was also caught up in World War Two, spending much of the war working on secret artillery fire control problems and cryptography at Bell Labs. That wartime research came with an important twist.

As the war drew to a conclusion in 1945, Shannon – with fellow Bell Laboratory scientists Ralph B. Blackman and Hendrik W. Bode – authored a paper entitled 'Data Smoothing and Predictions in Fire-Control Systems.' The authors likened the need to smooth raw data in fire-control system calculations to communication systems in which there was a need to separate a propagated signal from noise. Then, in 1948, Shannon co-authored a book with Warren Weaver, a mathematician who headed the Applied Mathematics Panel at the Office of Scientific Research and Development during the war. The book was entitled the *Mathematical Theory of Communication* and, with its publication in 1949, the Information Age was born. In subsequent years, Shannon earned the sobriquet "Father of Information Theory."

Network Infrastructure Through the Post-War Period

Aside from the use of science to advance telephony, there was the matter of the actual equipment. Strowger and other step-by-step switches represented an improvement in the state of the art, but they also had significant limitations. In improving both call handling and economic efficiency, new automation switching technologies would be critical. The crossbar switch would be the next big advance, incorporated several capabilities from the earlier panel exchanges, such as the internal checking of circuits, second call attempts and the annunciation of circuit problems. The initial design was the No. 1 Crossbar, or 1XB, and it was installed in Brooklyn, New York (in the Troy Avenue central office) in 1938.[3]

Designed for high volume urban areas, 1XB switches would often augment older panel switches within the same exchange. In the 1XB, a Line Link Frame (LLF) automatically connected outbound calls to a junctor (i.e., circuit), while a sender provided the necessary dial tone. Incoming call junctors provided a multiple wire connection between the trunk frame and the incoming call frame. Incoming and outgoing markers enabled the location of an available circuit, thereby simplifying and speeding up call setup and routing.[4]

The 1XB also broke new ground in two important areas. First, it could automatically apply alternate routing when necessary to avoid circuit congestion. In addition, the 1XB could route calls through non-consecutive private branch exchanges (PBXs). Although not very sophisticated by contemporary standards, he 1XB quickly proved to be effective and very reliable.[5] This was at the beginning of what we will call the Pre-Revolution era of telephony, during which successive generations of crossbar switching would become common. But telephone service was still far different from what it is today.

By 1941, Americans were able to make toll calls to distant cities. However, long distance calls were expensive and the call setup was time consuming. For example, a telephone call from the New York City metropolitan area to Chicago, Milwaukee or Kansas City might have taken over ten minutes to set up and complete the connection. Once connected, the analog voice transmission would not have had the same quality that modern telephony provides. With those analog transmissions the downline signal would be repeatedly amplified, but the amplification would continue the propagation of noise. Notwithstanding the advent of crossbar switches, American telephony remained tied to circa 1940 technology. After the December 7, 1941 attack on Pearl Harbor, the build out of the long distance infrastructure continued, but slowly due to wartime priorities. Nonetheless, an improved transcontinental telephone line was completed in December 1942. Then, right in the middle of the war, AT&T developed another switch that would prove to be a major advance in technology. Called a tandem switch (or, in old nomenclature, a toll switch), the new design was designated as a No. 4 crossbar, or 4XB. Under development since the late 1930s, the first 4XB was installed in Philadelphia during August 1943.

1938 image of a technician working at a No. 1 Crossbar switch in New York City. Courtesy of AT&T Archives and History Center.

The architecture of the 4XB was evolutionary. As a tandem switch, it could connect local circuits to long distance trunk lines or provide an AT&T "long line" trunk connection between distant cities. Unlike the earlier 1XB, the 4XB tandem switch would not provide a local connection to a user's telephone and, hence, it would not provide dial tones. No card translator boxes came with the early 4XB switches, so on most long distance (toll) calls operators used cordboards to complete a connection. However, due to wartime demands, further 4XBs would not be delivered until 1948.

The 4XB tandem was just an evolutionary advance in technology, but it served as a prelude to AT&T's Nationwide Operator Toll Dialing in the late-1940s. It was not a rapid process. Modern area codes (NPAs) would not appear until late-1947, and design of translation boxes to improve automation did not begin until 1949. In fact, it was not until 1953 that the original 4XB tandems were modified with translation boxes. These were metal punch cards that provided detailed call routing codes, including alternate routing instructions if the latter were needed to avoid congested circuits. In the intervening period when translation boxes were unavailable, hard code instructions within the switch provided default routing preferences.

Nationwide Operator Toll Dialing, once implemented, still relied heavily on operator assistance. A caller in Philadelphia who wanted to call a party on the west coast would still need an operator to set up the call. The operator would dial as many as twelve digits on a rotary dialer to set up the long distance call routing, followed by the local destination number – another four to seven digits. That was still a big improvement and, were it not for wartime priorities of labor, material and manufacturing facilities, more 4XBs would have undoubtedly been installed sooner.

The 4XB proved to be a highly reliable tandem switch; it would remain in service for nearly fifty years. AT&T's management clearly liked the crossbar switch technology, and the 1948 successor to the 1XB – the No. 5 Crossbar Switching System, or 5XB – would be equally successful. Unlike the tandem 4XB, the 5XB connected calls within a local area, and local numbers to an AT&T long line switch. As with the 4XB tandem, Bell Telephone Laboratories designed the 5XB, while Western Electric manufactured the hardware. The reliable 5XB remained in service well into the 1980s.

(Left) No. 4A Crossbar switch in Newark, New Jersey, taken during the 1950s. Note the size of the switch room. (Right) An engineer and technician at a

At this point, the importance of the Bell Telephone Laboratories deserves a special note. The introduction of the 4XB tandem occurred at a time when the laboratories were developing the top secret SIGSALY encrypted communication system for the military. Besides encrypted voice communications, SIGSALY established many other firsts in telephony, (e.g.) the first use of pulse code modulation (PCM); the first successful compression of voice bandwidth, and frequency-shift keying (FSK). Later on, FSK would reappear as an underlying technology in Caller ID. Audio frequency-shift keying (AFSK) would find uses in some of the early telephone modems. So wartime research and developments at the Bell Telephone Laboratories would often yield future benefits. Meanwhile, AT&T managed some improvements of its infrastructure during the war years, despite the constraints of time, labor and available funds. By the end of the war in 1945, the company had installed some 2,000 miles of coaxial cable in its system.

The Progression of Pre-Revolution Signaling

Telephone system signals enable telephone calls and, more recently, the transport of data services. In what we refer to as the Pre-Revolution era of telephony, methods of signaling depended on the very infrastructure that carried the voice call. It was much like commercial aviation before the arrival of jet aircraft.

You will recall that the very early magneto crank telephones had local exchange operators making wire connections at their office consoles. Early Strowger and other step-by-step switches were able to utilize simple pulsed digits; we will refer to them as subscriber pulses. Those early signals utilized direct current (d-c), and could terminate at a local office switchboard or a customers telephone, depending on the time and circumstance. As the early switchboards went through a series of upgrades, automation slowly encroached the telephone operator's turf.

The telephone itself was an important part of the signaling process; it is where many signals originated and terminated. After World War One, household telephones were commonplace and hand cranked magneto telephones gave way to rotary dial telephones. For outbound calls on a rotary-dial house phone, the experience began when the caller removed the receiver from the cradle and dialed the destination phone number. Each movement of the dial sent a pulse that represented a number from 0 to 9 into the system, and the resulting train of pulse codes would produce an address that would signal a particular telephone that there was an incoming call, thereby causing it to ring (an alert signal). The pulse train signals were nothing more than electrical pulses, and – along with the early step-by-step switches – represented an important step in automation, since the pulses would position the mechanical elements of the telephone switch. The prevalence of three and four digit telephone numbers during the first two decades of the twentieth century helped.

Especially in the early decades to the twentieth century, most were local and most telephone signaling was known as loop signaling. The nomenclature derived from the fact that the electrical pulses that originated on a home telephone were used on the local loop (i.e., connection) that existed between a subscriber's telephone and the local office exchange. A typical loop signal might have been a supervisory signal, indicating an "on hook" or "off hook" condition of a particular telephone. Early signaling systems could provide call progress signals such as a ringing signal, a busy signal, or an alert that all telephone circuits were unavailable. Telephone operators were still very much involved with connecting calls outside a local area, and it is the longer duration calls that best define the advances in signaling.

Calls that were carried outside the local area were routed by telephone "switches," a term that embraced both switch hardware and the physical office in which the equipment resided. Switch offices included local exchanges and long distance switches (often co-located); the current vernacular includes the generally interchangeable terms Mobile Switching Center (MSC) and Mobile Telephone Switching Office (MTSO). On calls that were routed over long distances, relay switches (i.e., tandem switches) were used. Tandems played an important roll in making long distance telephony practical. Even in the twenty-first century, tandem switches play an important role in call routing and impact the cost of making the call. But it is the arrival of crossbar switches in the late 1930s that serves as a useful (if imperfect) benchmark, because as significant advances in switch hardware appeared signaling continued to evolve. Of particular interest is Channel Associated signaling (CAS), which can be subdivided into the methodologies of inband and out-of-ban signaling.

With inband signaling, the telephone circuit that carried the analog voice signal also carried the call setup, control and teardown signals. This was a game changer for long distance calls, because signal tones were technically superior to predecessor systems and reduced the labor component of making such calls. Inband signaling functioned by superimposing either multi-frequency (MF) or singe-frequency pulses (SF) over the analog voice message. Analog telephone circuits use a frequency band between 0 to 4,000 hertz (Hz, or cycles-per-second), and the inband spectrum (in which the human voice propagates) runs from 300 Hz to 3,400 Hz. The methodology known as out of band signaling used the buffer zones at the upper and lower ends of that range, but mainly the frequencies between 3,400-4,000 Hz.[6] A frequency of 1,600 Hz for voice was initially used for inband signaling, although later on AT&T engineers moved the voice frequency up to 2,600 Hz for single frequency (SF), four-wire trunks, and either 2,400 Hz or 2,600 Hz for SF, 2-wire trunks.

The crossbar tandem technology and the regional 5XB switches all worked easily with inband signaling for both incoming and outgoing call traffic, as did 4XB toll switches. The early 1XB switches could handle incoming inband signals and, when using seven or ten digit MF pulses, could signal tandem switches that were set up for the new Automatic Message Accounting (AMA) and Automatic Number Identification (ANI) that began in the late-1940s. But before AMA and ANI were fully operational, the need for a better signaling system was becoming apparent. Dial tone signaling arrived during the 1960s, and that significantly improved the speed of call setup. Each button on the telephone produced a combination of tones, a much easier process than the rotary dial that preceded it. Tone dialing officially began on November 18, 1963 – four days before President John F. Kennedy was assassinated – and used a methodology known as dual-tone multi-frequency (DTMF). It took years before most telephones operated with DTMF tone dialing, and it still utilized the voice circuit for signaling.

DTMF, also known by the branded Touch Tone® name, would be the last major upgrade to MF signaling for domestic calls within the United States. Even in the SS7 era, DTMF would continue to be used for subscriber initiated signaling, although in the late twentieth century digital signal processors replaced tuned filter banks for decoding at the receiving end of the call. Signaling System 5 (SS5), also an inband MF system, was developed for the setup of international calls; it had no bearing on domestic call traffic within the United States.

SS5 was developed as a CCITT standard in 1964, and was often referred to as either C5 or CCITT Signaling System 5. Outside of the Bell Telephone System, CCITT protocols known as R1 and R2 existed from the 1950s-70s. R1 used MF tones in a CAS environment; it provided call and register signaling to private branch exchanges (PBXs) in the United States. R1 was also used in Japan. R2 was a CAS system that was widely used in Europe. R2 used a variation of MF signaling known as Multi-Frequency Compelled, or MFC.[7] Other changes in telephony began in the 1960s, including ten-digit dialing and the phase out of the two-letter prefixes in telephone numbers within the Bell Telephone System. With this overview, a closer look at postwar inband and out-of-band CAS is in order.

One of the problems with inband signaling was that the voice message and the superimposed signals could interfere with each other, despite the use of filtering. In fact, extraneous noise that was picked up during the conversation could be interpreted as a signal, sometimes resulting in a disconnected call. In addition, inband signaling was slow, and it tied up a considerable amount of bandwidth on the voice circuit. And inband signaling was susceptible to fraud. Frequency generators could be used to replicate signal tones in the voice circuit, which posed security and economic issues.

By the early 1970s, the activities of "phone phreaks" had become common public knowledge. These individuals would use whistles and other sound generators to impose signals into a telephone system, thereby seizing control of a trunk line for the purpose of making free long distance phone calls. The critical 2,600 Hz inband frequency was especially susceptible to seizure. The phreaks' activities were costly to telephone networks, and posed enormous security risks. One of the most famous phone phreaks used the pseudonym "Captain Crunch" since the famous Cap'n Crunch® cereal at one time came with whistles that could produce a 2,600 Hz signal tone.[8] So there were strong incentives for telephone companies to change to out of band signaling came into more widespread use.

Moving well above the 2,600 Hz frequency range enabled a signaling environment where filters were not needed, and provided important security advantages. Several trunk carrier channels were designed to accommodate out of band signaling at 3,700 Hz and, as a practical matter, signals in either direction would not interfere with the voice call. This technique worked better, although long distance calls sometimes passed through tandem connections. The normal bridge would require a d-c connection, but AT&T engineers had "through channel units" placed at the tandem connection. This architecture provided demodulation and then modulation of both the analog speech pattern and the 3,700 Hz signal tone, completing a nice a-c bridge and eliminating many issues associated with a d-c recovery across the tandem.

Despite the diligence of AT&T, Western Electric and the researchers at Bell Labs, using the voice circuit as the signaling medium, regardless of whether the signal transport method was inband or out-of-band, had limitations. For example, at the back end of the call the circuit would not be free until the line was cleared by the destination telephone receiver and the adjacent telephone switch. In fact, under scenarios where a receiver associated with the destination phone number remained "off the hook" the circuit would remain unavailable. And a plethora of other technical, security and economic issues that were endemic to Channel Associated Signaling remained.

Parallel Developments That Affected Telephony

Shannon and Weaver were not the only researchers at Bell Telephone Laboratories who made significant contributions to science. During the same early post-war period, physicists William Schockley, John Bardeen and Walter Brattain conducted experiments to find a replacement for the venerable, but expensive, vacuum tube. It was an important project. Ever since Lee de Forest invented the triode Audion, vacuum tubes had been an essential part of long distance telephony by functioning as amplifiers and relays.

But despite their valuable properties, vacuum tubes consumed considerable amounts of electric power and generated lots of heat. AT&T wanted a substantial improvement, and research was assigned to its Solid State Physics Group at Bell Labs Murray Hill, New Jersey campus. But on December 16, 1947, the researchers were stymied in their efforts to develop an adequate contact point. Brattain and Bardeen made a final attempt to develop a solution; they conducted an experiment with a germanium crystal that supported two gold contacts. This is known as a point-contact transistor, and with this combination their final attempt was successful.

On January 23, 1948, Schockley went still farther. Based on 1940 research by the physicist Russel Ohl, Schockley conceived of a transistor that functioned as a junction. This was accomplished by "sandwiching" N- and P-type germanium together; it was called a bipolar junction transistor (BJT). The newly invented BJT was multi-functional. It was, and is, an active electronic component that can amplify an electric current or signal, be used as a resistor and convert analog voice transmissions to a digit signal.

The BJT transistor was prominent in both discrete and integrated circuits until roughly 1980, after which CMOS technology became dominant in integrated circuit design. It would still be a few more years before transistors could be manufactured in quantity. Nonetheless, by 1949, the move away from vacuum tubes in telephony had begun.[9]

Besides William Schockley's junction transistor, 1948 saw another development that would affect telephony: i.e., the previously mentioned Automatic Message Accounting, or AMA. The concept behind AMA was to automate the labor-intensive process of gathering subscriber information for toll calls. It was designed to work with customer direct dialing (DDD), although initially an operator would come on the line to request the needed information for billing.

Automatic Number Identification, or ANI, provided the second part of the process, but neither system appeared quickly. AT&T used an operations plan that placed AMA operators in centralized regional offices (CAMA). This expanded customer direct distance dialing and eliminated the operator data collection function from local offices. However, the size of even the early post-war AT&T network was enormous, and it utilized a mix of equipment, including 4XB, 1XB and 5XB crossbar switches, plus a number of the earlier SXS switches. Chronologically, the implementation of AMA/CAMA did not begin until 1953, and continued well into the 1960s. Implementation of ANI also continued into the mid-1960s.[10]

In 1952, Charles Clos devised what came to be known as the Clos network. This was essentially a multistage circuit-switching network in which the number of circuit switched crosspoints could be reduced if the switching were accomplished in sequential stages. With sequential non-blocking stages, Clos published his mathematical proof entitled 'A Study of Non-blocking Switching Networks' in the March 1953 edition of *The Bell Telephone Technical Journal*. Dr. Václav E. Beneš, a Bell Laboratories mathematician, produced a permutation of the Clos network in which the interior stages are modified with additional crosspoints. That work was important, as was Beneš' work on non-linear filtering.

Then in 1961, John D. C. Little, at the time a professor at Case Western Reserve University, published a paper entitled 'A Proof of the Queuing Formula: $L = \lambda W$.' The queuing formula $L = \lambda W$, where L equals the long-term average number of customers (callers) in a stable system; λ equals the long-term average effective rate of arrivals, and W equals the average time duration that each customer (caller) remains in the system (i.e., waiting time) came to be known as Little's law.

Little's law attracted considerable attention from AT&T managers. His proof derived from, and restated, Erlang's $E = \lambda h$ formula, that was discussed earlier in this section. What's of interest here is that by 1961 the use of solid-state electronics was replacing vacuum tubes in the AT&T system. At this point AMA/CAMA and ANI were streamlining (to some extent) accounting and administrative functions on the network. Claude Shannon and Warren Weaver had delivered the Information Age, touch-tone signaling had arrived on handsets, but the underlying signaling system still utilized voice circuits as the medium for signaling.

In May 1965, the first No. 1 Electronic Switching System (1ESS) switch was installed in Succasunna, New Jersey. Voice telephone calls were still analog, and the essential signals that controlled call setup and supervision still traveled on voice circuits. However, ESS technology arrived two decades after the end of World War Two, at a time when the "baby boomers" and a growing population were driving call traffic to ever-higher levels. By 1968, AT&T operated roughly 1,600 long distance switching offices in the United States and Canada, and routed traffic through some 300,000 long-haul trunks. AT&T imposed its Switching Plan for Distance Dialing, of which its Automatic Alternate Routing (AAR) was a key component.

Technicians at work at the No. 1 ESS switch in Succasunna, New Jersey during 1965. Courtesy of AT&T Archives and History Center.

1ESS technology, like many other generational changes in telephony, did not happen quickly. Designed as a general-purpose switch, the 1ESS could perform the functions of the earlier 1XB and 4XB switches. As its design was being prepared for production in late-1964, it represented the largest project ever performed in-house for the Bell Telephone System.[11]

The 1ESS switch was highly redundant, as reliability was paramount. It was also the first Stored Program Control (SPC) switch to be manufactured in numbers, and included a central processor (CPU) with wired logic for basic information processing; a scanner and distributor for input/out functions, and a special stored

56

program for all switching tasks. The IBM 7094, around which the new system was designed, was a second-generation, transistorized version of an earlier vacuum tube mainframe.

The 7094 ran a tape-based operating system called IBSYS,[12] which was based on General Motors SHARE operating system; it was sometimes known by the rather unfortunate acronym SOS.[13] So transistors were part of the new switch system design, as were reels of tape and mechanical relays. With both line frames and trunk frames that used up to three types of junctors, old-fashioned reed switching fabric and a plethora of wire-spring relays, the new 1ESS switch would be able to handle up to 100,000 calls per hour.

Quiet Winds of Change

Many readers of this history were unborn as the 1ESS entered service during the 1960s, and were never able to experience telephone service as it existed back then. But the fact that different technologies and telephony protocols advanced at different rates is sometimes revealed in our popular culture. One familiar example is the 1973 film classic *American Graffiti*. The movie was set in the northern California town of Modesto in 1962, where its director George Lucas grew up. Near the end of *American Graffiti*, Curt Henderson (played by actor Richard Dreyfus) enters a radio station to request a song dedication. The then-famous disc jockey Wolfman Jack made an on-screen appearance, and broadcast the song dedication that night. In his broadcast, the Wolfman encouraged the lovely blonde who was driving a Thunderbird in Modesto to call his friend Curt at Diamond-3132.

So the 1960s, the decade in which 1ESS technology, manned space flight and telecommunication satellites arrived, still used telephone numbering protocols that were decades older than even the jalopies that cruised Modesto streets in 1962. Telephone switches had evolved, and electronics had moved from vacuum tubes to transistors. And so it was with signaling systems. Signaling remained circuit related (CAS), regardless of the frequency range of the signal. CAS also imposed limits on the technology, because of the deterministic relationship between the controlling signals and the voice messages. With CAS, signal tones would basically just set up calls, including the proper routing over trunks, and terminate the call – the latter a process that network engineers called "teardown." But then the 1970s arrived and, finally, telephone signaling was at the cusp of a major change.

◊   Notes on Further Reading   ◊

Some of you may be interested in further reading on topics that were discussed in this section. The side notes below provide a little more information and may stimulate some interest. But this is purely optional, and not necessary for those who feel no need for further reading about probability, math or logic theory.

◊   Side Notes on Poisson and Stochastic Processes   ◊

Probability is important to operational planning in any large-scale telephone system. System infrastructure requirements, labor needs, work schedules, budgets and operational plans are all heavily dependent on statistical analysis and probability. Many students who are not fond of algebra, geometry or trigonometry are nonetheless fascinated by concepts in statistics and probability.

The Poisson process is a continuous-time process for counting events. In telephony, it is necessary to evaluate the likelihood of such random things as traffic spikes so that equipment and personnel can be properly deployed. A Poisson distribution can be created from this process so that traffic engineers have a frequency distribution of possible events within a time interval. From their analysis an expected value can be derived for a random event that is of interest for planning purposes.

The Poisson process is a stochastic process, which means that the object of the study (e.g., calls into a local telephone exchange) is affected by random variables. The randomness of such a process is evidenced by the fact that there is no memory of prior events, circumstances or performance (outcomes). One important aspect of telephone system planning involves the queuing of calls during peak demand periods. Thus, the models that are created have applications in call queuing and call routing protocols within a particular system.

◊   Side Notes on Boolean Algebra and Logic (Gates)   ◊

Boolean algebra, also known as Boolean logic, was developed by the English mathematician George Boole (1815-1864). It was first promulgated in his 1847 pamphlet entitled *Mathematical Analysis and Logic*. This was followed by his 1854 book entitled *The Laws of Thought*. Boolean algebra has numerous applications in mathematics, logic and information theory.

Electrical engineers have an interest in what is called two-element Boolean algebra in applications such as circuit design. Typically, the integers 0 and 1 correspond to conditions of high voltage and low voltage, respectively. In logic, the integers 0 and 1 correspond to the false and true conditions, respectively. Many students will be familiar with truth tables, whereby for each variable that appears in an input column there are one or more possible outcomes. Logic gates are a typical application of truth tables, for which some examples are provided below.[14]

2-Input AND Gate	2-Input OR Gate	2-Input NOR Gate

Boolean expression:	Boolean expression:	Boolean expression:
$A \cdot B = Q$	$A + B = Q$	$A \downarrow B = Q$
(A AND B gives Q)	(A OR B gives Q)	(NOT A and NOT B gives Q)

Plain English:	Plain English:	Plain English:
Output Q will be true A and B are both	*Output Q will be true if either A or B is true.*	*Output Q will be true if A and B are both not true.*

Truth Tables

2-Input AND Gate	2-Input OR Gate	2-Input NOR Gate

A	B	Q	A	B	Q	A	B	Q
0	0	0	0	0	0	0	0	1
0	1	0	0	1	1	0	1	0
1	0	0	1	0	1	1	0	0
1	1	1	1	1	1	1	1	0

Section Two Footnotes

1 Note: Venn diagrams are a useful way to become familiar with Boolean logic, as not all readers will find further discussion of logic gates or other Boolean applications to be of interest. For those who are interested in further reading, online sources are generally a good starting point. Texts on Boolean algebra are appropriate for those who are interested in electronics, circuit design or college level mathematics.

2 The MIT article was the publication of Shannon's master's degree thesis at MIT, where he earned his advanced degree in electrical engineering. His faculty advisor was Frank L. Hitchcock. See URL:
   http://dspace.mit.edu/handle/1721.1/111733

3 Note: The Troy Avenue central office in Brooklyn. NY was the perfect test site as it would experience high call volume, but was in a convenient location for maintenance.

4 Note: Despite the numerous advantages, the 1XB technology arrived just as the Roosevelt Administration began to mobilize in advance of World War Two. The widespread introduction of new switch technology was therefore delayed until after 1945.

5 Note: Western Electric, the manufacturing arm of AT&T, licensed the technology from the Swedish telecommunications firm L.M. Ericson.

6 Out of band signaling at 3,700 Hz replaced 2,600 Hz, while in Europe the CCITT standard was 3,825 Hz for out-of-band signaling.

7 See 'Signaling Systems for Control Telephone Switching' by C. Breen and C. A. Dahlbom, published in *The Bell System Technical Journal*, Vol. XXXIX, No. 6, November 1960.

8 Note: The phreaker who was called "Captain Crunch" was completely unrelated to the cereal. Cap'n Crunch® brand is owned by The Quaker Oats Company, which was not involved in any phreaking efforts. For additional information on phone phreaks see the January 7, 2007 *Wall Street Journal* article entitled 'The Twilight Years of Cap'n Crunch' by Chris Rhoads, retrieved on November 29, 2012 from:

http://online.wsj.com/public/article/SB116863379291775523-_EQCu93LyjSommsN6J7qiCozuu8_20070122.html?mod=blogs.

9 In 1956, Schockley, Bardeen and Brittain received the Nobel Prize in Physics for inventing the transistor. In 1957, ten years after the transistor was invented, John Bardeen – then a professor of electrical engineering and physics at the University of Illinois (Champaign-Urbana) – joined with Leon Cooper and John Robert Schrieffer in proposing what came to be known as the standard theory of superconductivity, or BKS. For their work in BKS, Bardeen, Cooper and Schrieffer received the 1972 Nobel Prize in Physics.

10 See *Signaling System 7* (Fifth Edition) by Travis Russell, copyright © 2006 by The McGraw-Hill Companies, see p. 25 on Automatic Number Identification (ANI).

11 See 'No. 1 ESS: System Organization and Objectives' by W. Keister, R. W. Ketch-ledge and H. E. Vaugh, published in the September, 1964 edition of *The Bell Telephone Technical Journal*.

12 See IBM Systems Reference Library, File No. 7090-36, Form C28-6248-7, entitled 'IBM 7090/7094 IBSYS Operating System, Version 13, System Monitor (IBSYS), which document is a reprint of C28-6248-6 with updates, dated December 30, 1966, copyright © 1963 by International Business Machine Corporation.

13 Note: For additional research, see SHARE, Inc. Records, 1955-1994, Collection Number CBI 21, at The Charles Babbage Institute, University of Minnesota. Summary of the historical collection was retrieved on November 29, 2012 at: http://discover.lib.umn.edu/cgi/f/findaid/findaid-idx?c=umfa;cc=umfa;rgn=main;view=text;didno=cbi00021.

14 Image credit for the logic gate depictions above are as follows.

The AND gate ANSI symbol was drawn by jjbeard in 2006; the public domain source file is AND_ANSI.svg. AND_ANSI.svg was retrieved on November 6, 2012 from:

http://en.wikipedia.org/w/index.php?title=File:AND_ANSI.svg&page=1.

The OR gate ANSI symbol drawn by jjbeard in 2006; the public domain source file is OR_ANSI.svg. OR_ANSI.svg was retrieved on November 6, 2012 from:
http://en.wikipedia.org/w/index.php?title=File:OR_ANSI.svg&page=1.

The NOR gate ANSI symbol was drawn by jjbeard in 2006; the public domain source file is NOR_ANSI.svg. NOR_ANSI.svg was retrieved on November 6, 2012 from:
http://en.wikipedia.org/w/index.php?title=File:NOR_ANSI.svg&page=1.

Section Three

SS7 and Common Channel Signaling – A Better Nervous System

. . . SS7 networks consist of high-speed packet switches and dedicated circuits that are separate from, but inter-connected with, the tele-communications networks over which telephone calls are carried.

- Federal Communications Commission (FCC), Notice of Proposed Rulemaking, WUTC Docket Number UTC-980329, FCC 98-101

. . . Like the great American Revolution, the IP technology revolution will usher in a new form of democracy. It will place more and more control into the hands of individual citizens and away from central institutions. In short, technology is democratizing communications like never before.

- Prepared remarks of FCC Chairman Michael K. Powell at the 'Voice on the Net' conference at Boston, Massachusetts, held on October 19, 2004.

When significant changes in telephony signaling methods did occur, they did not begin in the United States. As with the nineteenth century telegraph systems, the major advances in signaling started in Europe, and not until 1972. That was later than might have been expected, given the advances in science and technology that had already taken place with telephony. But when it came, the changes in signaling were profound.

C6 – or CCITT Signaling System 6 – started the Quiet Revolution. C6 was the very first system to use what is known as the Common Channel Signaling (CCS) methodology. With CCS, signaling was removed from voice telephone circuits and placed in a completely separate infrastructure. By using CCS, C6 avoided tones and used data packets to propagate information; it could more effectively control a large number of voice circuits than any preceding system. Call setup and teardown occurred faster with C6 than with predecessor systems, and could return a cause code for a failed call. Significantly, C6's CCS architecture enabled the existing trunk line infrastructure to absorb the increased call demands of a larger, and more mobile, population. Yet in another way the C6 architecture was unusually simple: i.e., it was monolithic.

C6 was regarded as an improvement over the earlier C5 system that AT&T used to connect international calls, including those that used a satellite link. But despite its superiority, C6 was not quickly adapted in Europe.[1] In 1976, AT&T – recognizing the superiority of what they called Common Channel Interoffice Signaling (CCIS) No. 6 – inaugurated the system in the United States.[2] The launch of what is more commonly known as Signaling System 6, or SS6, went smoothly, and the methodology was soon extended to Canada. AT&T, along with other players in public telephone service and equipment markets, recognized that telephony was moving beyond what was called Plain Old Telephone Service, or POTS. AT&T's Network Planning Division published its document entitled 'Notes on the Network' in 1980, which superseded its earlier 'Notes on Distance Dialing.' AT&T's 'Notes on the Network' discussed Common Channel Interoffice Signaling (CCIS, which was the American nomenclature for CCS), which was still based on SS6 when the document was published in 1980. But event more changes were coming. SS6 used 28-bit signal unit and would not be usable for future needs. The use of telephone circuits for Caller ID, facsimile machines and dial-up modems would soon be commonplace, and AT&T system planners knew it.

You will recall from Section Two that ever since the publication of Shannon and Weaver's *Mathematical Theory of Communication*, network engineers had recognized that signaling systems were really information systems. SS6, with its monolithic architecture, had significant limitations that would adversely affect several higher order operations. In addition, SS6 had bandwidth and packet size limitations that would be insufficient for future network requirements. So Signaling System 6 was a big step forward, but it could only be an intermediate step. The stage was now set for Signaling System 7.

Telecommunications Standards

At this point, it is useful to look at the various organizations that have been responsible for setting telecommunications standards. One of the key players was an organization known as ITU, based in Geneva, Switzerland. ITU was established in 1865 in Paris, France, over a decade before Alexander Graham Bell applied for his famous telephone patent. The organization was originally known as the International Telegraph Union; it changed its name to the initials ITU in 1934. In 1947, two years after World War Two ended, ITU became a specialized agency of the newly formed United Nations (UN). This was a useful arrangement, since up to that time most telecommunication networks, either telegraph or telephone, were either owned by a national government or by companies that operated as government authorized monopolies. ITU's UN affiliation gave it an official status that was respected by governments around the world.

Due to the nature of telecommunication technologies and services, much of the work done by ITU was accomplished in committees. In 1956, two existing committees merged and formed the new Consultative Committee for International Telegraph and Telephone, or CCITT. By the 1980s, private ownership of telecommunication service providers ("telcos") and free-market competition often supplanted government-owned monopolies. Given the freer and more dynamic environment that was becoming increasingly common, the ITU's Plenipotentiary Conference rearranged itself during 1993 to be more responsive to changes in technology, market conditions and national policies. The result was three new divisions. Matters involving telecommunications standards ITU-T; matters involving telecommunications development came under the purview of ITU-D, while matters pertaining to radio communications came under the purview of ITU-R. The predecessor CCITT was replaced by ITU-T in the new reorganization.[3]

The above chronology is important to maintaining historical perspectives that pertain to the development of Signaling System 7. After years of discussing drafts, Geneva-based ITU published its first SS7/C7 recommendations in 1980; this was a dozen years before CCITT was replaced by ITU-T. The first publication was Q.700 ('Introduction to CCITT SS7'), which totaled 320 pages. All SS7/C7 documents are considered recommendations, providing the necessary flexibility for national authorities to establish their own variations of the generic standards. Interestingly, and despite the twelve-year interval between the first SS7/C7 recommendations and the establishment of ITU-T, CCITT only appears in the title of the original Q.700 document.

Once ITU-T was created, a subcommittee was established for the purpose of addressing matters that pertain to telecommunications signaling. That group was called Study Group 11, or SG11, and it operated under a broad mandate. Its recommendations continued the Q-series document lineage, and it studied signaling from a global perspective. In addition, it considered the state of existing technologies, regional and national regulatory frameworks and prerogatives, plus other matters such as performance, reliability and security. Note that the establishment of ITU-T and SG11 occurred just before the Internet and World Wide Web became major telecommunication entities. ITU-T's mandate thereafter extended to the Integrated Services Data Network (ISDN), including signal transport mechanisms.

The growth of the Internet and the World Wide Web also occurred as mobile telephones, and then modern cellular networks, evolved. By 2012, ITU had thirteen Study Groups and twelve regional offices in addition to its Geneva headquarters. Today, ITU-T issues recommendations that go beyond the traditional matters of telephone standards and include computer and Internet protocols.[4] The development of standards for mobile telephones usually begins in the European Telecommunications Standards Institute (ETSI), while Internet protocol standards typically originate in the Internet Engineering Task force (IETF).[5]

In 1990, another organization was born, this time in the United States. It was called the Inter-regional Telecommunications Standards Conference (ITSC). This evolved from the T1 committee in America, which invited ITU-T, ETSI and Japan's TTC to join. The goal of ITSC was to achieve greater international collaboration so that a consensus could be reached on standards issues. Unfortunately, the ITSC was too large and unwieldy for its intended purposes, so it morphed into the much smaller Global Standards

Collaboration (GSC). The GSC held its first conference in Melbourne, Australia in 1994 and, during the next several years, groups from other nations joined. In 2001, GSC named itself the Global Telecom Standards Collaborative (GTSC) and holds an annual meeting. Organizations such as the Telecommunications Industry Association (America), China Communications Standards Association and the Association of Radio Industries and Businesses (Japan) participate.

Of course, there are other groups that participate in standards discussions. However, the foregoing is a useful overview of the organizational framework in which telecommunications standards are established.

ITU-T SS7/C7 Standards Recommendations

You will recall it being mentioned that the first SS7/C7 standards recommendation was Q.700, and published in a document entitled 'Specifications of Signaling System No. 7 | Introduction to CCITT SS7.' While a complete reading of Q-series standards recommendations is not necessary, a sampling of selected documents is a good preparation for understanding how Signaling System 7 was designed. (Note that the actual documents use the European spelling of signaling with two 'l's, while in America signaling has just one 'l'. This mini-book utilizes the America spelling.) The old CCITT published standards documents in 1980, 1984 and 1988. In 1992, and thereafter, publications were issued by the ITU-T. When CCITT was publishing standards recommendations, each series was identified by a color. Hence, the 1980 edition was called the CCITT Yellow Book, 1984 was the CCITT Red Book, and 1984 was the CCITT Blue Book.[6]

The first ITU-T publication (dated 1992) was ITU-T Q.767, which dealt with International ISUP. Subsequent ITU-T publications have been called 'White Books' as the prior CCITT color-coding scheme was abandoned. In looking at the CCITT/ITU-T standards recommendations, we need to look back in time and bear in mind how different SS7 would be from the then fairly recent SS6. SS6 took signaling out of voice trunk circuits, but it was monolithic. SS7 would use protocol layers arranged in a stack. The CCITT followed the Open Systems Interconnection (OSI) model that was developed by the International Standards Organization (ISO).[7] This differed from the evolving TCP/IP standard for the Internet, a separate story that is not of immediate concern. Bear in mind that the very first work on what became OSI actually began in 1967, and well before either TCP/IP or the modern Internet even existed. The very first work on what became SS7 actually predated that by three years.[8]

So the development of SS7 was based on OSI layers, but of course OSI was still very new. Not surprising, the SS7 protocol stack architecture would evolve with the passage of time and the benefit of experience. When CCITT first published its Yellow Book in 1980, only the Message Transport Part 2 (MTP2), Message Transfer Part 3 (MTP3) and the Telephony User Part (TUP) existed. This is the big picture of what was happening, circa 1980. Q.700 is another excellent primer in the overall concept of how SS7/C7 signaling would work. Within Q.700 a reader is introduced to such topics as: signaling network components, OSI layering, signaling message structure; Message transfer Part (MTP) MTP addressing; Signaling Connection Control Part (SCCP) addressing, and signaling system performance.

A sampling of other Q.7XX standards recommendations for SS7 appears below: [9]

Q.701   Functional Description of the Message Transfer Part
Q.705   Signaling Network Structure
Q.710   PABX Application
Q.780   SS No. 7 Test Specification (General)

The SS7 Protocol Stack

The first (lowest) three layers of SS7 comprise the Message Transport Part of the hierarchy, and are referred to as MTP Layers 1 through 3. The lowest layer is MTP1, MTP2 corresponds to the physical layer of the generic OSI protocols

MTP1 is the layer that is tasked with the physical transfer of signal data through signaling links; think of it as hardware. Either a DSO-A or V.35 interface will be used, which are consistent with Bellcore (later Telecordia) and ANSI specifications.[10]

MTP2 corresponds to the data link layer of the generic OSI protocols, and is tasked with sending signal data from one node (i.e., junction) to the next one. MTP2 is concerned that signal messages are delivered in the correct sequence, and uses a sequential numbering scheme and length indicators to account for lost or out-of-order messages. MTP2 accomplishes reliability functions such as fault and error monitoring with CRC-16 error checking.

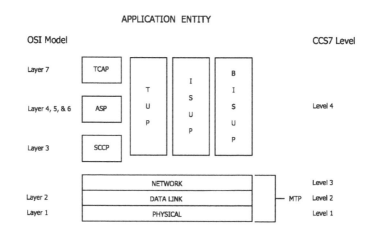

SS7 Protocol Stack

Below the heading CCS7 Level (upper right) are the SS7 levels that are used in the
United States. Note the subtle differences from the OS layers.

MTP3 corresponds to the lower part of the network of the generic OSI protocols; it is tasked with multiple functions. The MTP3 message discrimination function allows non-terminating messages to pass through the node. This includes the establishment of an alternate signal route if there is a fault within the signal network. It also routes local signals to their destination. MTP3 sends signal messages between nodes in the signaling network, such as Link Status Signal Units (i.e., LSSUs, sent via MTP2) to establish an alert of link failures. In addition, MTP3 performs diagnostic functions such as link realignment (i.e., traffic removed from link and counters are reset), resynchronization and other link management functions.[11]

Some attention to the OSI Layer 3 is now in order. OSI Layer 3 appears as a single layer in the OSI hierarchy, but it is equivalent to no less than three different layers of the SS7 protocol stack. As mentioned above, MTP3 corresponds to the lower portion of the generic OSI Layer 3.

Immediately above MTP3 in the SS7 stack is the SCCP layer. SS7's SCCP layer accommodates the Signaling Connection Control Part, and corresponds to the upper part of the generic OSI Layer 3. SS7's SCCP layer provides for complete signal message routing from the point of origin to the destination. In addition, SCCP ensures that TCAP messages get routed to the correct database.[12] The last of the three SS7 layers that corresponds to the upper part of OSI Layer 3 is called ISDN-UP. ISDN is the acronym for Integrated Services Digital Network, and UP stands for User Part. ISDN-UP combines the two acronyms. It is often referred to as ISUP.

ISUP is extremely important, as evidenced by the fact that its functions overlap OSI Layers 4, 5, 6 and 7. Essentially, ISUP was designed to replace the earlier Telephone User Part (TUP) and Data User Part (DUP) protocols. ISUP is used for call setup and teardown (i.e., ending the connection) functions. ISUP also controls other functions such as billing, call transfers, and determination of whether a voice channel will be used for a regular voice call, facsimile use or data transport. However, ISUP does not provide broadband services.[13]

As of early 2012, TUP was only being used in China. ISUP is primarily used in North America, and facilitates the connection and disconnection of local telephone offices in the PSTN. In addition to ISUP, the Asynchronous Transfer Mode (ATM) exists as a transport mechanism for voice as well as signaling channels. However, ATM has not replaced ISUP. For example, the ISUP is still used for specific functions, such as sending decoding instructions to the terminating switch.

TCAP stands for Transactions Capabilities Application Part and, like ISUP, it sits above the three Message Transport Part layers. TCAP handles what may be referred to as ancillary services. For example, TCAP supports essential network functions such as translation and database transactions. When an external database is queried, SS7 receives a TCAP reply. For telephones that use Message Waiting Indicators (MWI), TCAP is what enables handset annunciation. TCAP can also serve as a transport mechanism for upper level SS7 activities. In particular, TCAP can access and activate features in a different switch.

TCAP has proven to be an extremely versatile protocol, and can significantly improve the economic efficiency of a network. One example of this versatility is the use of SS7/TCAP as the transport mechanism for Short Message Systems (SMS), which deliver text messages. This practice by telecom networks significantly reduces their capital expenditures because they can use SS7 and TCAP instead of a far more expensive 3G broadband infrastructure.[14] Another example is the use of TCAP and SCCPs to communicate the Mobile Identification Number (MIN) that is associated with a subscriber's mobile telephone number, the latter being more formally known as a Mobile Directory Number (MDN). This is critical to Local Number Portability (LNP) and call routing, especially when a handset user is roaming outside of a subscriber's home area. We will discuss roaming in greater detail a little later.

MAP stands for Mobile Access Part and, like TCAP, it corresponds to an upper level OSI layer (usually 6 or 7). MAP, which is only used in cellular networks, is very important since it enables one network to communicate with other networks using SS7. MAP can also provide the Electronic Serial Number (ESN) or Mobile Electronic Identification Number (MEID) to another network through an SS7 link.[15] As you are no doubt aware, cellphone users often move about, often outside of their home area. As a result, communication with the Home Location Register (HLR) is critical, and this is enabled by SS7. When position information about a roaming handset is communicated to or from the HLR, TCAP forms the transport mechanism and MAP resides above it. You can no doubt appreciate the importance of maintaining service as the handset user moves bout, and the MAP is central to that capability.

OMAP is the acronym for SS7's Operations, Maintenance and Administrative Part. Like MAP, which it appears next to in the SS7 protocol stack, it corresponds to upper level OSI layers. OMAP uses the TCAP protocol to provide communications and control capabilities from a remote location.[16] Although most telephone service subscribers are unaware of it, network administrators and senior executives actively monitor and control landline and cellular networks. This is critical when a natural disaster or some other major event either spikes calls or renders a portion of a network unusable.

BISUP is another term that is frequently encountered; it is the acronym for the Broadband ISDN User Part. The broadband capability made BISUP far superior to the earlier and slower ISUP. However, as networks evolved during the 1990s the Asynchronous

Transfer Mode (ATM) protocol also came into play. ATM provided broadband services such as high definition video, streaming images and digitized voice. BISUP traffic could run on the ATM, with the Signaling ATM Adaptation Layer (SAAL) replacing MTP2. However, the continued evolution toward IP-based telephony solutions impacted ATM as well as ISUP/BISUP. In 2005, the fourteen-year old ATM Forum began a series of mergers, and in 2009 ended up as part of the Broadband Forum. However, SS7 remained alive and well at PSTNs, in which signaling remained a critical and evolving function.[17]

SS7 Nodes and Links

Although SS7 has been designed with impressive capabilities, much of the architecture is quite simple. This can be seen in the three main components. They are the Service Switching Point(s) (SSP), the Service Transfer Point(s) (STP), and the Service Control Point(s) (SCP). These components are known as "nodes" or signaling points. In a schematic or network diagram, nodes appear as junctions.

The Service Switching Point (SSP) is a telephone system switch.[18] We have been discussing switches from the early Strowger switches of the 1890s to the Crossbar series that mostly appeared in the 1940s, and then the Electronic Switching System (ESS) technology that appeared in the 1960s. You may also recall from our prior discussions that word switch can refer not just to an individual switching device (like a No. 4 Crossbar, or a 1ESS electronic switch), but to the facility in which physical switches, backup power sources and personnel are housed. The switch facility, which is what we are usually referring to when we discuss call routing, typically occupies several thousand square feet within a telephone company building. Having this mental picture may be useful if you look at a simplified signaling system diagram.

The Service Transfer Point (STP) is a packet switch that sends and receives signals (i.e., coded digital messages) between telephone network switches, a database computer, so some other signaling junction (node). An STP, because of its importance, also acts as a network hub.[19] It is helpful to remember how this arrangement differs from earlier signaling. One of the reasons that SS7 was developed was to move the signals away from the circuits that carry the telephone message. STPs usually have a mate so they can operate as connected pairs, albeit from separate locations. This provides a level of redundancy that is essential to any telephone network.

The Signal Control Point (SCP) is basically a centralized computer database that can respond to queries from SSPs. Having centralized data storage is desirable in that all SSPs have access to the same information; that stored information should be up to date. SCPs eliminate the expense and potential of having a local database that is not up to date. SCPs often operate in pairs, with each being in a separate location to ensure redundancy.[20]

Remember that SSPs, STPs and STPs are considered SS7 functions. As such, they may be fulfilled at the physical location of a node within a company's SS7 network, such as a switch. Also note that each individual signaling point has its own unique point code, or address. When a signaling message is sent from one signaling point to another, an originating and a destination point code will be embedded within the message. Signaling points all use a routing table to ensure that the preferred routing path is used to deliver the signal over the desired path. That signal roadway is formed from links. Now, let us look at the various types of links that can connect SS7 nodes.

One really nice thing about the way that SS7 links are organized is the simplicity. There are six types of links, each type described by noun nomenclature and a letter. Their functions are pretty straightforward, as indicated below.[21]

Access Link (A-Link)   Access links connect a signaling end point (SEP) to a Signaling Transfer Point (STP). The SEPs will be either an SSP or a SCP.

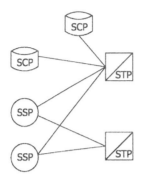

A-Links

Bridge Link (B-Link)   Bridge links connect a Signaling Transfer Point (STP) to another STP. They link is called a bridge because it typically denotes a connection in which one or more STPs bridge to peer STPs. Often the "bridge" is to their peers in another network. Sometimes you will see this described as a B/D link, since a bridge link can also be considered as a diagonal link (discussed below).

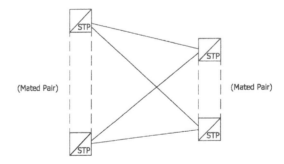

B-Links

Cross Link (C-Link)   Cross links are used to solve a particular problem. When an STP becomes isolated from a signaling destination due to one or more link failures. In this situation an STP may be linked to an STAP that performs the identical function. Thus, the cross-link enables the two STPs to operate as a mated pair, thereby enabling a signaling message to be sent to the desired destination. Note: There are situations in which an SCP may be paired with an equivalent SCP. However, in this scenario there is no direct link connection between the two SCPs.

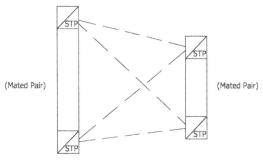

(Mated Pair)   (Mated Pair)

C-Links

Diagonal Link (D-Link) Diagonal links connects a pair of secondary STPs to a primary pair of STPs.

Extended Links E links connect an SSP to an alternate STP. This would

(E-Link) occur if the link between the SSP and its regular, or "home" STP, failed.

Fully Associated Link
(F-Link) Some networks do not have Signal Transfer Points (STPs). In those cases, any communication between signaling end points (SEPS, which in this case would be SSPs and/or

75

SCPs) would be a fully associated link.

Now that we know about SS7's three basic components and six fundamental links, let as look a bit further into SS7 architecture. You will recall that in 1976, once Common Channel Signaling (CCS) came into being with SS6, that the actual path of signal messages was removed from the voice trunks altogether. So with both SS6 and SS7, it is helpful to visual a separate and somewhat parallel network. With what is now known about nodes and links, we can begin to visualize the CCS framework of Signaling System 7.

Beginning with a local telephone switch, a voice telephone call will travel to a switch in the destination area, often passing through one or more tandem switches enroute.[22] At the first switch, we will place a Signal Switching Point (SSP). A signal message that includes typical call setup and routing information is sent by an access link to the associated Signal Transfer Point (STP). Lets say that the next node will be the Signal End Point (SEP), which happens to be the SSP at the destination switch. Another access link will deliver the message from the STP to the destination SSP. This simple route is an example of the quasi-associated signaling mode, which is common in the United States.

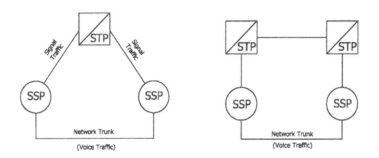

Quasi-Associated Signaling Mode (left) and Non-Associated Signaling Mode (right).

The foregoing information is sufficient to give you a general idea of how Signaling System 7, with its Common Channel Signaling (CCS) architecture, differs from the earlier Channel Associated

Signaling (CAS). Hold onto those concepts as we briefly look at other matters that affect the availability of SS7 for public switched telephone networks (PSTNs).

An Interim Look: Companies, Regulators and the District Court

When U.S. District Judge Harold H. Greene entered his Modification of Final Judgment (MFJ) on August 24, 1982, the full impact of Signaling System 7 had yet to be revealed. At that point the focus of national attention was on the breakup of AT&T and the new competitive landscape that would soon appear. Within the constellation of events and conditions that evolved, the cost of SS7 and the ability of smaller telecoms to access it became major concerns.

Prior to the breakup of AT&T, the long distance carrier operated for many decades as a regulated monopoly. AT&T had the capacity to invest hundreds of millions of dollars (and more) into network infrastructure, something that much smaller forms could not match. A look at the competitive landscape is useful.

On January 1, 1984, as a direct result of Judge Greene's rulings, seven Regional Bell Operating Companies (RBOCs) were created. Originally referred to as Regional Holding Companies, the RBOCs were completely separate business entities. The new Regional Bell Operating Companies, or "Baby Bells" were: Ameritech, Bell Atlantic, BellSouth, NYNEX, Pacific Telesis, Southwestern Bell and US West. Let us take a moment and look at these, and other, post-divestiture companies.

Ameritech was formed in 1983 and was based in Chicago, Illinois, leasing space above the Chicago Mercantile Exchange. Ameritech served as a holding company for five legacy Bell Telephone Company subsidiaries in the upper Midwest, and also owned Ameritech Mobile Communications, LLC.[23] The latter company was the nation's first public provider of mobile phone service; it was later renamed Ameritech Cellular. However, the breakup of AT&T and the Telecommunications Act of 1996 did not always go smoothly. It heralded a number of new mergers and acquisitions, as the new companies sought to achieve critical mass in a more deregulated marketplace. That was evident in 1999 when Ameritech merged with Dallas-based SBC Communications.

The merger of Ameritech with SBC Communications was an important consolidation of resources in the post-divestiture marketplace, but it came with considerable scrutiny. Both federal and state regulators were very concerned that the merged company's pricing power would be excessive, so one requirement was that Ameritech Cellular sell its assets to GTE Corporation. GTE (formerly General Telephone & Electronics Corporation) was the largest independent telephone company in the United States, and it was felt that their acquisition of Ameritech assets would ensure adequate competition. A final condition required the post-merger SBC Corporation to provide local service in thirty markets outside its home area by April 2002. Federal and state regulators were determined that in the aftermath of a regulated national monopoly, competition had to be effective.[24]

Bell Atlantic was another one of the "Baby Bells." The regional telecom operated several subsidiary telephone companies in an area that extended along the eastern seaboard from New Jersey to Virginia and westward through Pennsylvania. In 1996, Bell Atlantic merged with New York-based NYNEX and retained the name Bell Atlantic for the merged company; it was headquartered in New York City. In June, 2000, Bell Atlantic acquired GTE in a $52 billion merger and adopted the name Verizon Communications, Inc.[25]

The morphing of the new Bell Atlantic into Verizon Communications through the GTE merger, significant as it was, was not the only major change the affected the new firm during 1999-2000. The company that came to be called Verizon Communications had a big interest in cellular communications. Bell Atlantic and a firm called Air Touch had participated in a joint called Primeco; this partnership involved mobile telephones. Air Touch was a 1994 spin-off from Pacific Telesis (a Baby Bell), and was absorbed by London, England-based Vodafone Group PLC in June 1999.

Vodafone, founded in 1991, was one of the world's largest mobile phone telecoms, second only to China Mobile as of 2011. In September 1999, less than three months after it absorbed Air Touch, Vodafone formed a partnership with Bell Atlantic to create a large, U.S.-based cellular network. The new business was Cellco Partnership, and combined Bell Atlantic's existing subsidiary called Bell Atlantic Mobile with Vodafone AirTouch's United States operations.[26] Verizon Communications, Inc., best known today as the wire-line telecom and provider of FiOS cable and high-speed Internet service, would own 55% of Cellco Partnership, with the remaining 45% being owned by Vodafone. The new partnership is best known to consumers by its trade name of Verizon Wireless.[27]

At this point, it is clear that the telecommunications industry had become embroiled in the entropy of a new regulatory environment. The disorder accompanied the change from a regulated monopoly to a more customer oriented, competitive market. The legislative intent of the Telecommunications Act of 1996 was to improve service and lower customer costs through real competition and technological innovation. What lawmakers did not visualize was the imposition of new costs that would flow from the demands of inter-carrier traffic, local number portability, and the practice of cellphone users to roam outside of their home area. Actually, lawmakers did not have to visualize or even anticipate all of these changes, since the power of the FCC to oversee the new marketplace was left intact. Before long, the disparate structure of new costs emerged and became manifest in inter-carrier tariffs.

In 1996, Common Channel Signaling technology had been in existence for more than two decades. Not all carriers purchased SS7 hardware, software and softswitches. The major hurdle, especially for smaller telecoms, was cost. SS7 was expense to deploy, and while the superiority of its database connectivity and signaling was not in doubt, the cost of implementation would adversely affect a carrier's earnings. Smaller carriers sometimes purchased SS7 services from vendors, and that became a good – albeit imperfect – solution.

But another factor entered into the calculus of SS7 deployment. Beginning in 1984, toll-free "800" calling arrived, and business customers demanded it. The new service would generate billions of dollars of revenue, something that no major carrier could ignore. Yet toll-free "800" dialing was only possible with SS7. So even before the new regulatory landscape emerged in 1996, and despite the high cost of deployment, economic necessity pushed the telecoms into SS7. And with that, the Quiet Revolution was underway

SS7 and Local Number Portability (LNP)

With the passage of the Telecommunications Act of 1996, the FCC imposed a mandate for Local Number Portability (LNP) on

American telephone companies. This was a huge change that came with daunting technological consequences, and it applied to all service providers in the 100 largest Metropolitan Statistics Areas (MSAs).[28] Before the arrival of LNP, changing carriers was relatively infrequent. Yes, there was some competition before LNP, as many local markets were served by both a Baby Bell (i.e., an Incumbent Local Exchange carrier, or ILEC) and one of smaller, independent providers (i.e., Competitive Local Exchange Carrier, or CLEC). But when a customer changed carriers, he or she would relinquish their existing telephone number. LNP changed all that.

The 1996 arrival of LNP occurred when most Americans utilized wireline (land line) telephones, and it was SS7 that made the implementation of LNP possible. But that having been said, it was the proliferation of mobile phone devices that benefited the most from SS7. LNP may have enabled phone service subscribers to change carriers, but cellphone users added another dimension to telephone service: i.e., roaming. To appreciate why telephone service as we know it today became dependent on SS7, we need to look at the twin benefits of number portability and roaming.

You may recall from Section Two that a digital revolution led to the Information Age, the latter being associated with the work of Dr. Claude Shannon – author of the 1949 book *Mathematical Theory of Communication*. Both LNP and roaming are highly dependent on databases and systems that can work with databases, and this can easily be seen in methods of call routing.

For a typical telephone service subscriber, information needed to originate a call would typically be stored at a nearby switch facility. Remember, in telephony the word switch refers to a physical entity: i.e., a building (or portion thereof) that would house equipment such as circuit switches, electrical buses, computers and backup power sources. In the Public Switched Telephone Network – or PSTN – a switch would be associated with a local telephone exchange. But after LNP arrived in 1996, both routing information and routing methodologies changed. Information about the routing of ported numbers would be stored in a new database – i.e., an LNP database. The new LNP database would be administered by an independent company.

The big changes that LNP introduced into telephony were preceded by another important event – the portability of toll-free numbers assigned to area code 800. SS7 enabled business users to switch from one carrier to another and keep the same toll-free 800-numbers. That was possible because SS7 made database access and call routing information available in a fast and practical way. Once the portability of toll-free 800-numbers became an established methodology, the move to LNP was just an incremental step, albeit an important one.

Let's look at a call that might have been placed after LNP came onto the scene in 1996. A preliminary step in connecting that call would be a query by the local exchange (i.e., a Class 5 switch) to the LNP database. This represented a sea change in the methods of telephony for residential and business customers who had not benefited from the portability of 800-numbers. The query would reveal if the number being called had been ported; if so, a local routing number (LRN) would be provided to the originating switch. The originating switch would then use the 10-digit LRN to route the call to the destination switch. For this reason, LRNs are sometimes referred to a "steering digits." [29]

Now, do you remember our earlier discussion of the SS7 protocol stack? You will recall that just above the MTP3 layer of the Message Transport Part is the SCCP layer (Signaling Connection Control Part). The query to the LNP database is possible because of the SS7 Transaction Capabilities Application Part (TCAP) and SCCP. Without SS7, the database query could not be made, and the local switch would not know how to route the call.

Next, let's look at the above-mentioned LRN. In old-fashioned Plain Old Telephone Service (POTS), the local switch that originated a call would simply use the digits of the destination number to route the call.[30] After the arrival of LNP, if the call under discussion was made to a number that had not ported out, the call would still be routed using the digits of the destination number, and the originating switch would have the preferred routing. However, the actual routing would follow an LNP data base query, which every call would generate.

While a query for every call might seem time consuming and wasteful, American telecoms decided that due to operational considerations that practice – known as "all call query" – was preferred. Of course, for ported numbers the LNP database would provide the LRN that would be used for call routing. That LRN would identify the switch to which the call would be routed, and the network path over which it would be routed. Upon arrival at the destination switch the LNR would no longer be needed; the actual area code and number, and not the LNR, would then be used to complete the call.

SS7, Caller-ID and Other Features

Because of SS7's ability to connect and interact with databases, a number of new opportunities emerged. One of them, Caller ID, actually preceded LNP by several years. Modern day telephone subscribers consider Caller ID to be *de rigueur*, yet it did not come into common use until the early 1990s. Caller ID is part of the ISUP protocol, and is an example of the signaling system communicating information not to a network entity, but to a phone user.[31] With Caller ID (the incoming call number) comes the availability of Caller Name, which requires a separate look up in a database once the number of an incoming call is established. Caller-ID is important to most consumers, but it is not the only example of a network signaling system interacting with the actual customer.

One of the more recent uses of SS7 is that of enabling the very popular ringback tones (RBTs). RBTs are usually (but not always) music that is played to the calling party after a connection has been made. SS7 provides call routing information (i.e., through the 10-digit area code and phone number, or the LRN), enabling the call to be connected to the switch near the destination. As you already know, telephone switch facilities can access numerous databases. In what is essential a three-part process, the destination switch first recognizes that the subscriber has selected the RBT option. The switch then queries a database to determine what the RBT selection (usually which song) the calling party should hear, and then establishes an IVR port connection so that the desired tone can bee played. (The same process applies if a message is to be played.) Once the caller answers the call, the IVR drops of the line and the call proceeds.[32]

One point that should be made here pertains to database management. SS7 can be fully functional, but it does not – and cannot – manage databases. One area where database errors often affect a subscriber is with Caller-ID. When a call connection is established, SS7 knows the numbers that are associated with the calling party and the receiving party. Sometimes a receiving party sees the caller's telephone number, but it is tagged with an incorrect name. This problem often generates a call to the telecom's customer service center, whereupon a correction to the database must be made. Here, a glimpse behind the scenes is useful, as the solution to an incorrect name is to update and correct the database.

The name database operates much like the LNP database, and network access is provided through a Service Management System (SMS, not to be confused with the SMS acronym that refers to the Short Message System for text messaging).[33] Some telecoms outsource this database function to other companies, which saves money but adds a degree of complexity when errors have to be corrected. Correcting the database involves having that company the "owns" the error impose the correction. As a result, a caller who makes a complaint with customer service may be asked to direct that complaint to carrier that can update the caller name database. Even then, imposing an individual fix immediately is problematic since the databases are 'bulk loaded.' The databases are updated frequently, so fixes can be made even though real-time corrections are not possible. A corrected name that is to be associated with a particular phone number will appear after the subsequent bulk load to the name database has been completed.

SS7, the HLR, VLR and Roaming

The rapid expansion of cellular service in the 1990s presented new challenges for telecoms. Subscribers, no longer constrained by a wireline connection, could now take their cellphones and travel throughout the country. While roaming around the country, as long as a cellphone user had a national service plan and could make a network connection, he or she would expect to have service. You have already learned that databases have become an integral part of modern telephony, and that is especially important with cellphone users. For each subscriber, information about the subscriber must be maintained in a database and, for cellular service providers, this is called the Home Location Register (HLR).

The HLR database is under the control of the home area to which a particular number is assigned. The switch facility is known, alternatively, as a Mobile Telephone Switching Office (MTSO) or Mobile Switching Center (MSC). The HLR data is used for both call routing and billing and, when updated, has reasonably current information about the cellphone's most recent location.[34] However, because the HLR database is not dynamic, its information is limited to the identity of MTSO that controls the area in which the subscriber is roaming, and the routing instructions to that MTSO. Only the Visited Location Register (VLR) will have updated information about the particular cell tower that the handset is using. The VLR gets updates because the cellphone will send out a signal regularly, and that location information enables proper call routing when the handset is used outside of the home area.

Remember our earlier discussion of the SS7 protocol stack? Above the Message Transfer Part is the Transactions Capabilities Application Part (TCAP), which is used to handle ancillary services. In the instant matter, TCAP's ancillary services involve establishing and maintaining the signal connection for sending the most recent location information from the VLR back to the HLR; the actual information is carried in the Mobile Access Part (MAP). This way, the HLR will be able to use recent location information when queried about a call routing scheme.

A final point needs to be made, and that's about roaming. The term roaming describes the use of a cellphone outside of its home area. Back in the 1990s, many cellphone users had local or regional plans that restricted the geographic area of service. Of course, most cellphone users can now roam anywhere in the United States, constrained only by suitable coverage. A point needs to be made about the nomenclature that relates to roaming. Simply put, customers tend to think of the financial consequences of roaming, and that differs from the technical aspect. Technically, once the handset is used outside of its home area, it is roaming – even it if homes off a tower of the subscriber's own service provider. In the twenty-first century, most carriers have agreements with other carriers so that within the United States roaming charges do not apply, regardless of whose tower a user is homing off. There are exceptions, of course, a common one being situations near the U.S.-Canadian border, where an American subscriber may home off a

Canadian tower. But for our discussion in this mini-book, we will be referring to roaming in a technical sense only: i.e., a cellphone user does not incur any roaming charges, but does move around outside his or her home area. And seamless roaming, plus SS7 and the build out of cellular network infrastructure, made twenty-first century wireless networks ubiquitous.

◊   Thoughts for Non-Science/Engineering Readers   ◊

By now, you have noticed that the story of SS7 includes a number of technical and scientific terms, plus numerous acronyms. Please remember that this mini-book was designed to meet the needs of a very diverse readership. But for those with interests and backgrounds in non-technical areas, your needs are just as important as the future engineer. So in your case, just getting a sense of what technicians and engineers deal with is all that you need. Many tens of thousands of former waiters/waitresses, bus drivers, retail clerks and others have found satisfying jobs at telecommunications companies. They need people with a wide variety of skills (including good people skills). One of them may have a place for you!

Section Three Footnotes

1   Note: C6 is often regarded as a circa 1972 signaling system, and was less widely used than the predecessor C5. Significantly, C6 was based on pre-OSI architecture although it did have shorter delay intervals after the dialing was completed. However, it should be noted the OSI was originally conceived back in 1967, an important point for dating the technology. Source: correspondence with Travis Russell regarding the origins of OSI. See also the online version of 'Pre-SS7 Systems' published by Cisco Press, copyright © Cisco, Inc. It was placed at the SS7.net domain with written permission from Lee Dryburgh and retrieved from the web address below on November 6, 2012: http://www.ss7-training.net/sigtran-training/ch04lev1sec1.html.

2   Note: As a useful benchmark, the inauguration of SS6 by AT&T was roughly concurrent with the 1976 inauguration of the 4ESS digital electronic switch. Source: AT&T Archives.

3   Note: The International Telegraph and Telephone Consultative Committee acquired the acronym CCITT from the French derivation Comité Consultatif International Téléphonique et Télégraphique. See also 'ITU's History,' retrieved on November 6, 2012 at:
http://www.itu.int/en/history/overview/Pages/history.aspx.

4   Ibid web source.

5   See 'About ETSI,' retrieved on November 6, 2012 at:
http://www.etsi.org/website/aboutetsi/aboutetsi.aspx.

    See also 'About the IETF,' retrieved on November 6, 2012 at:
http://www.ietf.org/about.

6   See 'History of SS7,' Table 4-1: Timeline of CCITT/ITU-T SS7 Timeline, retrieved on November 6, 2012 at:
http://www.ss7-training.net/sigtran-training/ch04lev1sec2.html.

7   Note: The Open Systems Interconnection (OSI) standard was largely developed by the International Organization for Standardization (ISO, based on the Greek word for 'equal' [isos]) and documented in ISO/IEC 7498.

8   Source: correspondence with Travis Russell.

9   See 'History of International Telephony Standards,' Table 2-1: ITU Core/Traditional C7 Recommendations, retrieved on November 6, 2012 at:
http://www.ss7-training.net/sigtran-training/ch02lev1sec1.html.

10 Note: V.35 is classified as a high-speed serial interface for Data Communications Equipment (DCE).

11 See *Signaling System 7* (Fifth Edition) by Travis Russell, copyright © 2006 by The McGraw-Hill Companies, see p. 120-125 for OSI and MTP-1/2/3; p. 107 for LSSUs, p. 113 for TCP/IP and TCAP, and p. 115-116 for LSSU link status and link failures.

12 Ibid, see p. 126-128 for SCTP and SCCP, p. 466 for SCCP in ANSI networks; p. 467-468 on SCCP service levels, and p. 469-472 on SCCP routing and flow control.

13 Ibid, p. 128.

14 Ibid, p. 130.

15 Ibid, p. 659.

16 Ibid, p. 108 on OMAP use of TCAP, and p. 109 on OMAP as a user of TCAP and the ASN-1 syntax standard.

17 Note: ATM was not intended to be a replacement for SS7. Because MTP was designed for the TDM environment, it was not suitable to handle IP or ATM channels. This resulted in the development of ATM as a different transport mechanism for SS7. Source: correspondence with Travis Russel. See also *Signaling System 7* (Fifth Edition) by Travis Russell, copyright © 2006 by The McGraw-Hill Companies, p. 320 on ATM technology, BISUP, SS7/TCAP and the planed Advanced Intelligent Network (AIN). See also the Broadband Forums' 'About the Broadband Forum,' retrieved on November 6, 2012 from:
http://www.broadband-forum.org/about/forumhistory.php.

18 See *Signaling System 7* (Fifth Edition) by Travis Russell, copyright © 2006 by The McGraw-Hill Companies, p. 62-63 on SSPs.

19 Ibid, p. 63 on use as an SS7 router for SSP traffic using MTP or TCP/IP protocols.

20 Ibid, p. 66-71 on SCP functions. Note also that SCPs may sometimes not be paired. For example, HLRs may very well not be paired due to the high cost that would result. Source: correspondence with Travis Russell.

21 See *Cisco SS7 Fundamentals*, 'SS7 Signaling Architecture' by Cisco Systems, copyright © 1992-2012 by Cisco Systems, all rights reserved. Retrieved on November 6, 2012 from:
http://www.cisco.com/en/US/products/hw/switches/ps2246/pr oducts_pre-
installation_guide_chapter09186a00800ea6d1.html#xtocid8.

22 Note: with multiple trunk switches, the signaling has to be set up between every switch along the route. ISUP signaling only deals with one switch at a time, although ISUP does provide the destination information. Source: correspondence with Travis Russell.

23 Note: Ameritech Mobile Communications, LLC survives as a holding of AT&T Mobility. Along with its corporate structure, the technology also changed over the years. Ameritech originally used code Division Multiple Access (CDMA) technology, but after absorption by SBC Communications (later AT&T Mobility) is switched to Time Division Multiple Access (TDMA). The AT&T cellular networks used a version of TDMA known as IS-136 before migrating to the GSM standard.

24 Note: There was a potential $1.18 billion fine if the local service requirement were not met. See FCC 99-279, CC Docket No. 98-141, Memorandum Opinion and Order, adopted October 6, 1999.

25 See FCC 00-221, CC Docket No. 98-184, 'In re Application of: GTE Corporation, Transferor, and Bell Atlantic Corporation, transferee,' Memorandum of Opinion and Order, adopted June 16, 2000.

26 See FCC Action by the Chief, Wireless Telecommunications Bureau, and Chief, International Bureau, March 30, 2000. FCC action was taken by issuance of separate Memorandum of Opinion and Orders (DA 00-721 and DA 00-730).

27 Note: Not to be confused with the publically traded majority owner, Verizon Communications, Inc. having NYSE symbol VZ.

28 See FCC 96-286, 'In the Matter of Telephone Number Portability 95-116,' CC Docket No. RM 8535, First Report and Order and Further Notice of Proposed Rulemaking, adopted June 21, 1996.

29 Note: When a customer switches carriers, the MDN will remain the same but the MIN (LRN) will change.

30 Note: Within the United States, callers should be aware of the demise of 7-digit dialing. Under the North American Numbering Plan 10-digit dialing is expected to become universal, even for most local calls.

31 Note: Prior to the capability of accessing databases, Caller ID was not possible.

32 See *Signaling System 7* (Fifth Edition) by Travis Russell, copyright © 2006 by The McGraw-Hill Companies, p. 8 and p. 646 in ringback tones.

33 Ibid, p. 22, 68 for Service Management System.

34 Ibid, p. 7, p. 333 on HLRs.

Section Four

SS7's Environment: SONET, TCP/IP and SIGTRAN

An SG is a signaling agent that receives/sends SCN native signaling at the edge of the IP network. The SG function may relay, translate or terminate SS7 signaling in an SS7-Internet Gateway. The SG function may also be co-resident with the MG function to process SCN signaling associated with line or trunk terminations controlled by the MG (e.g., signaling backhaul).

- Excerpt from an October, 1999 memo by the Network Working Group of The Internet Society. The references above pertain to Signal Gateways (SG), Switched Circuit Networks (SCN) and Media Gateways (MG) in the SS7 environment. Source memo: 'Framework Architecture for Signaling Transport,' copyright © The Internet Society (1999). All rights reserved.

When Common Channel Signaling (CCS) arrived in America during 1976, it was in the form of the somewhat limited SS6. Also somewhat limited was the state of the art of fiber optics, another technology that would soon change telephony in a big way.

Fiber optic technology had actually existed for some time. In 1880, four years after he received his United States patent for the telephone, Alexander Graham Bell tested a device that was called a photophone. The photophone actually worked – it could carry human voice transmissions, but it was severely range limited. The apparatus itself was pretty simple: i.e., speech (or other sounds) modulated reflected sunlight, which was directed by a mirror into a cylindrical channel. At the receiving end of the channel was a parabolic mirror that connected to a vibrating diaphragm and selenium resistors. Because of the inverse relationship between the resistance of crystalline selenium and the intensity of the light, modulated light became a workable medium for the propagation of voice and other audible signals. So despite its limitations, Bell's device was a precursor to what would appear a century later.

Now, let's fast forward to the late-1970s. By that time fiber optics had arrived, and the pluses and minuses of analog and digital modulation were well understood by radio and traffic engineers. Digital signals had signal to noise ratios that were superior to AM and FM analog signals, and noticeably better multichannel capabilities. But weighing against digital signals was the high cost of equipment at both the transmitting and receiving end. So fiber optic communications did exist, but significant limitations remained for a long time. As a result, telecom networks continued to rely on their effective and reliable coaxial cables. But that would eventually change.

The big advance that permitted fiber optics communications to leap ahead was an emerging technology known as Dense Wavelength-Division Multiplexing (DWDM). DWDM evolved from the earlier Wavelength Division Multiplexing (WDM) technology, which began to appear in the early 1980s.[1] WDM operated in the Infrared (IR) portion of the frequency spectrum, and it opened the door to additional bandwidth solutions. The development of Coarse Wavelength-Division Multiplexing (CWDM) and DWDM followed, but the latter had the advantage of being able to utilize far more Infrared (IR) channels. DWDM also involved the use of a multiplexer at the transmission site and a demultiplexer at the receiver site.[2] This was ideal for telecoms, since they would be able to increase traffic capacity (bandwidth) on a limited amount of cable. Consumers would reap huge advantages from the improved bandwidth capabilities but, as you might imagine, there was another hurdle that had to be crossed.

By the early 1980s, different telecoms were using a plethora of different fiber optic systems, the result being numerous issues with incompatibility. So in 1984, just as U.S. District Judge Harold Greene was issuing his landmark rulings that broke up the AT&T system, the Exchange Carriers Standards Association (ECSA) proposed new interconnection standards for fiber optic infrastructure.

SONET

During 1985, Bellcore advanced the interconnection standards concept a little further, and their proposal led to what came to be known as SONET. SONET is an acronym that stands for Synchronous Optical Networking, and it became formalized when the American National Standards Institute (ANSI) approved the new standards in 1988. SONET standards cover the local electrical portion of the signal (called STS, for Signal Transport Signal), while the Optical Carrier Level portion (OC) covers the signal that gets transmitted over fiber optic cable.[3]

The availability of SONET provided several significant advantages to telecoms. First, it was an advance of asynchronous signal transports methods. Asynchronous data transport is a methodology in which individual terminals within a network utilize their own clocks; there is a lack of synchronization. With SONET, multiplexing and demultiplexing message traffic is far simpler. Going beyond that, SONET enables interconnections of terminals that would otherwise not be possible. That's an important advantage, because different manufacturers build terminals with different line rates (i.e., measured in Mb/s), and the rate differences can be significant. And of course, there was a huge increase in bandwidth.

The magic of SONET did not fix one issue, however. Synchronized fiber optics greatly improved message transport capabilities, but it constituted the physical backbone of a telephone network message delivery infrastructure. Also needed was a message delivery protocol that would enable telecoms to move far beyond Plain Old Telephone Service (POTS) and into the unified realm of voice, data and video message delivery. ISUP (the ISDN-User Part) was only capable of working with Time Division Multiplexing (TDM) channels that would be found in the PSTN. What was needed was the capability to work with channels in the previously mentioned Asynchronous Transfer Mode (ATM) circuits. That solution was to replace ISUP with a protocol to serve the Broadband ISDN, and that is called BISUP.

ATM, which was first conceived as a backbone technology in the late-1960s, uses cells to transport voice and data messages. The ATM cells consist of a 5-byte header and a 48-byte payload, the latter being a compromise that was reached with European interests. ATM became popular in the early 1990s, and remains in use in the second decade of the twenty-first century. Still, telecoms were moving towards something faster and better.[4] They found it in TCP/IP.

TCP/IP

TCP/IP (Transmission Control Protocol/Internet Protocol) was a big advance in Internet protocols. Along with the availability of SONET, TCP/IP provided telecoms with an alternative to legacy switching equipment and control methods. The benefits would include lower costs, improved performance and increased network capability. This all derived from the fact that the information transport and control functions were becoming integrated. You will recall our earlier emphasis that as a signaling system, SS7 could work effectively with databases. The most effective way to access and transfer data is with digital packets of data, which is exactly what SS7 does today.

What is now referred to as TCP/IP first appeared in a May 1974 IEEE paper entitled 'A Protocol for Packet Network Intercommunication,' authored by Vint Cerf and Bob Kahn. The lower lever IP functions and the higher-level TCP functions were later separated. However, it wasn't until the fourth version of the Internet Protocol – IPv4 – that there was widespread acceptance of a packet-switched protocol version. IPv4 is a connectionless protocol that was outlined in the Internet Engineering Task Force's RFC 791, which was entitled 'DARPA Internet Program Protocol Specification.' As a point of interest, RFC 791 was prepared in September 1981 by the University of Southern California's Information Sciences Institute (at Marina del Rey, California) for the Defense Advanced Research Projects Agency's Information Processing Techniques Office.[5]

The packet-switched link layer for which IPv4 was developed is the lowest layer of the Internet Protocol Suite. This includes Local Area Network (LAN) protocols like Ethernet, in addition to framing protocols such as the Point-to-Point Protocol (PPP). IPv4 functions as a "best effort" methodology that does not guarantee message delivery or proper sequencing; these are handled by the upper layer protocols such as TCP. Although it has been superseded by IPv6, IPv4 encountered address exhaustion in early 2011 due to the limitations of its 32-bit addresses. IPv6 was deployed commercially in 2006, but as of 2012 IPv4 remained the most prevalent version in worldwide use.

In reading about TCP/IP, readers mainly need to be aware that references to either IPv4 or IPv6 refer to the lower layer. In addition, be aware that the physical layer in the OSI model does not exactly match the TCP/IP link layer, as the latter is of greater scope. Of course, the increased emphasis on data transport by carriers ensured that the migration towards an IP environment would accelerate. But while TCP/IP is used on the Internet to support such things as the World Wide Web, email and file sharing, it has limitations that adversely affect its use for telephony, including data transport. Telephony in the twenty-first century would be migrating towards an IP-based environment, and that would affect switching. SS7 would still have to support PSTN legacy wireline infrastructure, plus cellular 2G/3G technology and call routing, in addition to data transport. To do that, SS7 would have to change.

Switching would also have to change. With the development of SONET, the transition to ATM for message transport, and the evolution to TCP/IP this was to be expected. In Section Two we talked about the advances in switch technology during the middle third of the twentieth century. Just as the 4XB and 5XB brought about important improvements in the state of the art, the contemporary movement towards an IP-based telephone environment saw the introduction of softswitches into the network infrastructure scheme. But what exactly is a 'softswitch'?

Softswitches for an IP Environment

The key to the softswitch nomenclature is the word 'soft.' You are no doubt familiar with software, be it your computer's operating system or applications software. We will now extend the software concept to switches. Let's be clear – there is still a physical building housing electrical buses, routers and switch equipment. But instead of circuit switching and call routing with either an LRN or the actual area code and number, a softswitch uses IP addresses and then routes the voice or data telephone call to an Internet destination. Moreover, every part of the message, be it voice or bits of data, are sent just like anything that you would send on the Internet.

Unlike the Internet, the softswitch works within a telecom network's infrastructure and provides many protections and services that are not available when you email someone. For example, IP-based telephony using TCP/IP still provides authentication and other security parameters that are not available when you email someone from your computer. This needs to be emphasized, because within the telephone network security remains a critical concern – just the opposite of what's often encountered in the wilderness of the Internet.

Softswitches, like their legacy predecessors, are pretty interesting. In fact, just having a little knowledge about these devices could lead some of you to an interesting career. Just remember, a softswitch is going to do much of what a legacy circuit switch did, but with Internet routing and signaling. Signal engineers often refer to softswitches as signaling engines that are capable of VoIP protocol conversions and intelligent call routing in a TCP/IP environment.

In addition, softswitches in telecom switch offices (MTSOs, or MSAs) typically provide media proxy support and fail-safe, physical connections from the switch chassis to the PSTN network.[6] And some softswitches are capable of handling SIP registration, wholesale billing, AAA server functions and even external API support.[7] By operating in an IP environment, the softswitch enables IP-based telephony to function with more seamless call routing and an improved use of available bandwidth.

Important Secondary Tasks

One thing that hasn't been discussed yet is the use of SS7 for secondary tasks, such as marketing, administration and billing functions.[8] This is an appropriate time to mention these items, because as the network becomes more capable an ever larger plethora of services and capabilities come into play. One major item is cost control. Keeping costs under control is essential for any telephone network. A network's cost structure affects both the profitability of the carrier and its ability to offer competitive prices. A major part of cost control in network operations is a practice known as Least Cost Routing (LCR), which refers to the methods used to route and deliver voice and data calls in the most economical manner.

In legacy PSTN infrastructure, the cost of establishing a line connection through tandem switches of other networks has been a big cost driver. LCR involves the selection of a routing path that avoids expensive toll charges from other carriers, even if the route itself is more circuitous.[9] Now, with ever "smarter" networks, softswitches with sophisticated routing algorithms ensure that each call is sent via the most cost-effective route.

LCR is not the only example of SS7 enabling management to protect both the carrier and its subscribers. Telecoms utilize special servers, often referred to as AAA servers, to fulfill authentication, authorization and accounting functions.[10] Authentication is a security function, so authentication practices are designed to verify the identity of network users. Authorization means that a particular user is allowed to utilize a given service, often by merely verifying that (e.g.) there is no "block" on a particular service. Accounting is also important. If network users are not properly billed for services a cost results, and that burden is passed on to everyone else.

AAA servers have typically used a client/server protocol that is best known by the acronym RADIUS, which stands for Remote Authentication Dial In User Service. It is common to have a RADIUS client at a Network Access Server (NAS), Virtual Private Network (VPN) servers, network switches and remote Access Servers.[11] RADIUS was first developed in 1991, but more recently a much improved successor has been designed. That successor is called DIAMETER, a pun since a diameter is equal to twice a radius – solid evidence that network engineers and management nerds are not without a sense of humor. And whereas RADIUS uses UDP [12] as the Internet transport layer, DIAMETER is designed to use TCP or SCTP (Stream Control Transmission Protocol), and offers even greater security and reliability.[13]

SIGTRAN

This all brings us to SIGTRAN, which is essentially SS7 over IP. The word SIGTRAN is an acronym for Signal Transport, and it was introduced in an October 1999 memo entitled 'Framework Architecture for Signaling Transport.' The paper was prepared by the Network Working Group of The Internet Society, and its contributors included such prominent equipment vendors as Nortel

Networks, Siemens, Telecordia, Cisco Systems and Lucent Technologies. Tekelec was also deeply involved; it developed a predecessor to SIGTRAN and offered it to clients and developers. The memo set forth the both the architectural framework and functional requirements that would be needed for migrating signaling systems to an IP environment.[14]

The evolution of SIGTRAN was both concurrent and congruent with the evolution of SS7, and the working group articulated several important points. For example, it was explicitly noted that within IP networks, TCAP signaling would accommodate information transfer between the SS7 domain and the IP domain as (e.g.) from the SS7 network to a Media Gateway Controller (MGC)[15] or Service Control Point (SCP), or from an SCP that resides in the IP domain to an SS7 network element.[16] So with SIGTRAN, the SCTP acts as a peer to the Internet's TCP. If you use a network carrier to provide any form of media, this may be of interest to you. For that reason, and to better understand how SS7 works in a SIGTRAN environment, a brief description of some of the new terms will be helpful. Let's start with media gateways (MG) and media gateway controllers (MGC).

The MG is a translation device or service that acts as an interface between otherwise incompatible networks and protocols, such as SS7, PSTNs and IP. MGs are often described as dumb terminals, and it might be helpful to think of them that way. However, an associated media gateway controller (MGC) is anything but dumb; it controls how the media gateway (MG) operates. Media Gateway Control Protocol Architecture was addressed by the Network Working Group of the Internet Society in an April 2000 memo entitled 'Media Gateway Control Protocol Architecture0 (see RFC 2085; document copyright © The Internet Society, 2000). The memo stated (in part):

> *Under the control of a Media Gateway Controller (MGC),*
> *the Media Gateway (MG) realizes connections. .. A Media*
> *Gateway (MG) function provides the media mapping*
> *and/or transcoding functions between potentially dissimilar*
> *networks, one of which is presumed to be a packet, frame*
> *or cell network. For example, an MG might terminate*
> *switched circuit network (SCN) facilities (trunks, loops),*
> *packetize the media stream, if it is not already packetized,*
> *and deliver packetized traffic to a packet network. It would*

perform these functions in the reverse order for media streams flowing from the packet network to the SCN.[17]

MGC protocol architecture evolved very nicely as telephony entered the twenty-first century. By 1998, interface parameters were established whereby the MG portion of the interface was married to the public switched telephone network (PSTN), while the MGC resides within the IP environment. This philosophy is what led to the circa 2000 memorandum by the Network Working Group which introduced the Media Gateway Control Protocol Architecture. Bear in mind that the protocols that govern media gateways are considered device control protocols, while protocols that deal with call/data connection control (e.g., SIP – for Session Initiation Protocol, or H.323) are signal protocols, and work with SS7. And in the hierarchy of protocols, device control operates in a lower-level master-slave relationship, while control (signal) protocols such as SIP, H.323 and H.248 function in a peer-to-peer relationship.[18]

AIN/INAP	MAP	IS41	ISUP		TCAP
TCAP					
SCCP					
MTP-3B	MTP3			M3UA	SUA
SSCF		M2PA	M2AU		
SSCOP	MTP2	SCTP			
AAL5		IP			
ATM	MTP1	Ethernet			
Physical Layer					

SS7 / SIGTRAN Protocol Stack

Note the position of the Ethernet immediately above the physical layer, and TCAP, IS-41 and ISUP above the SCCP layer.

You can probably appreciate that by enabling the migration of telephone systems to the Internet, data services and VoIP telephony (using bits of data) became possible, with significant economic advantages for both networks and consumers. By the way, don't get bogged down with the nomenclature. A media gateway controller (MGC) is sometimes referred to as a 'call agent' or by the now familiar term 'softswitch.' A good example of a softswitch that acts as a call agent is Cisco's PGW-2200 SS7/C7 Softswitch (formerly known as the VSC-3000). For those of you who may wish to study controllers further, some additional reading on SIP, various H-series protocols, and Real Time Protocol (RTP) will be extremely useful. But as a general point for all readers, the transition from switched circuit networks (SCN) to IP-based voice telephony has been, and remains, a long-term process.

Getting back to actual SS7 messaging within MGC domains, SIP will be the key; to some extent it will supersede SS7. SIGTRAN is enabling IP-based protocols to replace the earlier Message Transfer Part (MTP), which was designed for legacy Time Division Multiplexing (TDM) protocols. If you take a look back at the SS7 protocol stack, you will note the three basic Message Transfer Part layers: i.e., MTP1, MTP2 and MTP3. However, as SIGTRAN began to be implemented in circa 2000, some of the SS7 protocols were displaced by SIGTRAN protocols. SIGTRAN protocols were addressed in an October 1999 memo (RFC 2719) that was promulgated by the Network Working Group of the Internet Society. Entitled 'Framework Architecture for Signaling Transport' (copyright © The Internet Society [1999]), the memo identified three core components of the SIGTRAN protocol stack: [19]

a. SCN Adaptation Layer (protocols are M2PA, M2UA, M3UA and SUA);
b. Common Signaling Transport: i.e., Stream Control Transmission Protocol (SCTP), and
c. Standard IP Transport Layer.

A few final notes about SIGTRAN may be useful before we move on. First, SCTP was a big step forward for SS7 because with it, SIGTRAN was able to smoothly send peer-to-peer signals in the IP environment. In essence, SCTP enabled SIGTRAN to upgrade the CCS capabilities of SS7 as telephony migrated to IP-based solutions for both voice and data transport. Among other things, SCTP permits multi-homing, which is the capability of having one end point connect to numerous IP addresses. Besides functional advantages, this provides redundancy that is critical to SS7. SCTP also accommodates multi-streaming, and PSTN services in the IP environment. With SS7 being augmented with SIGTRAN protocols, the migration to SIP trunking and IP-based telephony will continue.

Section Four Footnotes

1   Wavelength-Division Multiplexing (WDM) involves the propagation of lasers having different frequencies within a single strand of optical fiber. The discrete optical signals are distinct due to the differing wavelengths and, for that reason, bidirectional multiplexing can be achieved. Dense Wavelength-Division Multi-plexing uses amplified signals in the C band (1525-1565 nm) or L band (1570-1610). See 'WDM Optical Communication Networks: Progress and Challenges' by Biswanath Mukherjee, *IEEE Journal of Selected Areas in Communications*, Vol. 18, No. 10, October, 2000. Copyright © Institute of Electrical and Electronic Engineers (IEEE), 2000.

2   Note: DWDM systems utilize terminal multiplexers and demultiplexers, along with optical add-drop multiplexers. The WDM frequencies at spaced at 100 GHz intervals, while DWDM is spaced with intervals as low as 25 GHz. See ITU-T G.694.1: 'Spectral Grids for WDM Applications: DWDM Frequency Grid,' retrieved on November 6, 2012 from:
    http://www.itu.int/rec/T-REC-G.694.1/en.

3.   Note: SONET optical carrier (OC) transmission rates are based on a digital signal bitstream, for which the base rate is 51.84 Mbit/s. Just multiply the OC numerical suffix by the base rate to calculate the bitstream. For example, OC-3 = 3(51.84 Mbit/s).

4.   Note: The majority of ATM networks use the Private Network Node Interface (PNNI) protocol, which utilizes a shortest-path-first algorithm for routing selection. The decline of ATM over time is evidenced by vendors who have shown a preference for other technologies, both in product lineup ad in the availability of support. ATM had

some good characteristics, such as the capability to establish virtual circuits statically or dynamically.

5. Author's Note: RFC 791 is worthwhile reading for any student of the Internet. For one thing, it shows the national defense imperative of the various protocols, as it was prepared for DARPA. It also clearly articulates how the function of the Internet Protocol is to enable to movement of datagram's through interconnected networks utilizing names, addresses and routs., and discusses the relationship of protocols. See also RFC 1349 and RFC 2474. Visit: http://tools.ietf.org/html/rfc791.

6. Note: Interconnects are typically ports like a DS-1/DS3.

7. Note: SIP registration is important due to technological trends. An external API (Application Programming Interface) can support uses such as SMS and other private sector activities that improve the customer experience and drive revenue for the carrier.

8. Note: In the evolution of telephony, SS7 enables network executives to better know the habits of their customers. Note that SS7 rather than switch information is the most complete, timely and useful information about subscriber habits.

9. See *Signaling System 7* (Fifth Edition) by Travis Russell, copyright © 2006 by The McGraw-Hill Companies, p. 644 on switch query of routing database for LCR.

10. Note: AAA functions are critical to network operations, and that importance is not properly appreciated. Those with an interest in working for a network may want to examine this further. A good starting place would be the Request For Comments (RFC) documents on the Internet Engineering Task force. For example, RFC 2619 is entitled 'RADIUS Authentication Server MIB' (Management Information Base). For those interested in a telecom career, some knowledge of both RADIUS and the later DIAMETER client/server protocols would be extremely useful.

11. Note: The IETF notes that in some scenarios, a RADIUS authentication entity might perform both client and server functions. Hence, a RADIUS proxy would have to support both the client and server Management Information Bases (MIBs). See RFC 2619 on RADIUS Authentication, which was retrieved on November 6, 2012 from: http://www.ietf.org/rfc/rfc2619.txt.
Source/Copyright note: RFC 2619 entitled RADIUS Authentication Server MIB,' copyright © The Internet Society (1999), all rights reserved.

12. Note: UDP stands for 'User Datagram Protocol,' and enables a datagram mode of packet-switched interconnections of networks. UDP is a "bare bones, "best effort" transport methodology with no "handshake" between the sender and receiver. This was one of the longstanding issues with the RADIUS protocol. See RFC 768, entitled 'User Datagram Protocol,' which was retrieved on November 6, 2012 from: http://tools.ietf.org/html/rfc768.
Source/copyright note: RFC 768, entitled 'User Datagram Protocol,' copyright © The Internet Society (1980), all rights reserved.

13. Note: Pat R. Calhoun, Glen Zorn and Ping Pan developed the initial DIAMETER protocol version in 1998. DIAMETER provided substantially improved transport and security over the predecessor RADIUS. RFC 3588 articulated the salient points of the IETF DIAMETER AAA technology; it has been superseded by RFC 6733. The earlier RFC 3588 was retrieved on November 6, 2012 from: http://tools.ietf.org/html/rfc3588
Source/copyright note: RFC 3588, entitled 'Diameter Based Protocol,' copyright © The Internet Society (2003), all rights reserved.

14. Sources: correspondence from Travis Russell. See also RFC 2719 entitled 'Framework Architecture for Signaling Transport,' copyright © The Internet Society (1999), all rights reserve. Retrieved on November 6, 2012 from: http://www.ietf.org/rfc/rfc2719.txt.

15. Note: The IETF issued RFC 2805, entitled 'Media Gateway Control Protocol Architecture and Requirements' in April 2000. This technology was actually implemented by H.248 (Megaco), which supports a wide range of networks. RFC 2805 was retrieved on November 6, 2012 from: http://tools.ietf.org/html/rfc2805.
Source/copyright note: RFC 2805, entitled 'Media Gateway Control Protocol Architecture and Requirements,' copyright © The Internet Society (2000), all rights reserved.

H.248 Version 3 was developed in Sept 2005, and published by ITU-T as H.248.1, entitled 'Gateway Control Protocol: Version 3.' See 'Gateway Control Protocol: Version 3, was retrieved on November 6, 2012 from: http://www.itu.int/rec/T-REC-H.248.1-200509-I/en.
Source/copyright note: H.248.1, entitled 'Gateway Control Protocol: Version 3,' copyright © ITU (2006), all rights reserved.

16. See *Signaling System 7* (Fifth Edition) by Travis Russell, copyright © 2006 by The McGraw-Hill Companies, p. 20 on SCPs and the replacement of application servers; p.66-71 on SCP interconnection functions; and p. 125 on SCP and IP addresses, and p. 472-473 on SCP point codes in SCCP messages.

17. Ibid footnote 15.

18. Note: SIP stands for Session Initiation Protocol. See *Signaling System 7* (Fifth Edition) by Travis Russell, copyright © 2006 by The McGraw-Hill Companies, p. 2, p. 20 and p. 44 for SIP description.

H.323 signaling is an ITU-T recommended standard for audio-video (AV) content that is transmitted over different network types, such as PSTN, IP or ISDN. It follows ITU-T Recommendation Q.931. Q.931 was retrieved on November 6, 2012 from: http://www.itu.int/rec/T-REC-Q.931/en.

In addition, for a detailed look at SIP, see (in its entirety) *Session Initiation Protocol: Controlling Convergent*

Networks, by Travis Russel, copyright ©2008 by The McGraw-Hill Companies. For an expansive look at IMS, see (in its entirety) *The IP Multimedia Subsystem: Session Control and Other Network Operations*, by Travis Russell, copyright © 2007 by The McGraw-Hill Companies.

19. See IETF RFC 2719, entitled 'Framework Architecture for Internet Signaling,' October 1999. RFC 2719 was retrieved on November 6, 2012 from:
http://www.ietf.org/rfc/rfc2719.txt.
Source/copyright note: RFC 2719, entitled 'Framework Architecture for Internet Signaling,' copyright © The Internet Society (1999), all rights reserved.

Section Five

SS7, Cellular Networks and the Consumer

.. complexity is the primary mechanism which impedes efficient scaling, and as a result is the primary driver of increases in both capital expenditures (CAPEX) and operational expenditures (OPEX). The implication for carrier IP networks then, is that to be successful we must drive our architectures and designs toward the simplest possible solution.

- Excerpt from RFC 3439, entitled 'Some Internet Architectural Guide-lines and Philosophy,' published by the Network Working Group of The Internet Society, copyright © The Internet Society (2002). All rights reserved.

Bundled and VoIP service related complaints increased by more than 11% this quarter, from 1,661 to1,847...Wireless telecommunications complaints increased by more than 9% from 29,390 to 32,124, with Call or Message to Wireless Device-related complaints comprising the bulk of the complaints in this category.

- From the FCC Quarterly Report of Consumer Inquiries and Informal Complaints for Fourth Quarter of Calendar Year 2011, released on February 14, 2012.

Not that long ago, cellphone users who traveled outside their home area faced significant service limitations. For one thing, cellular networks as we know them in the twenty-first century did not exist. The 1980s saw early development of a market for cellular carriers when the FCC began issuing licenses. The process began with lotteries, but these were abandoned in favor of simultaneous auctions. The hodge-podge development of an industry continued throughout the 1980s and -90s, with cellular subscribers being somewhat tied geographically to their provider.

One problem that cellular carrier users had to contend with was caused by the very mobility that was much touted. Even with geographically limited service plans, subscribers would often move around – and sometimes outside of their service area. But even within the subscriber's home area, changes in position created two related technical issues. The first issue was that of handoffs from one cell tower to another as the position changed; the second issue was the reuse of a particular radio frequency in other nearby cell towers.

Frequency reuse was simplified by the practice of not reusing a particular radio frequency on an adjoining cell tower. The minimum distance for frequency reuse could easily be determined by the formula $D = R(3N)^{0.5}$ in which D was the minimum separation distance, R was the cell tower effective radius, and with N representing the number of cellular antennas is each cluster.[1] Handoff standards were more complicated, although the techniques for "hard" and "soft" handoffs improved over time.[2] Along with the build out of the cellular infrastructure and improvements in technologies, information sharing was an important part of the huge success of cellular telephony. SS7 remained out of the public view, but was right in the middle of the important changes involving signaling and database access.

Even with improved handoffs and proper frequency allocation, one of the biggest challenges in cellular technology was the ability to roam without significant difficulties. Although what's called "seamless" roaming is now taken for granted, that was not always the case. In the 1980s and -90s, the many cellular carriers were arranged like feudal fiefdoms. During the 1980s, as the FCC auctioned wireless licenses, the World Wide Web didn't exist, and the Internet was just evolving from the predecessor ARPANET.[3] In fact, it was during 1982 that TCP/IP [4] was established as the Internet Protocol Suite. Four years later, the National Science Foundation (NSF) granted research institutions and universities access to NSFNET,[5] and by the late-1980s Internet service providers began to open up commercial access to the Internet. SS7 preceded all of this, and so did X.25.

X.25 evolved from the ARPANET and packet switching.[6] The latter was a 1960s methodology that could form a single logical network from disparate physical network entities. Packet switching was integral to ARPANET, providing significant speed and bandwidth advantages, along with routing capabilities that increased transport reliability. It was from this experience that X.25 was developed in 1974, two years before the somewhat limited SS6 arrived in the United States.

X.25 had its debut in England, where it was used to develop the SERCnet[7] educational and research network. In 1978, X.25 Packet Assembler/Disassemblies (PADs)[8] were used on the International Packet Switched Service (IPSS), a network that started in both Europe and the United States, but grew to extend around the world. X.25 was highly regarded by its users, and not surprisingly it found its way into new uses. Telenet [9] deployed X.25 in its early Telemail email service, as did CompuServe when it introduced email to PC users at home in 1979. Financial institutions found X.25 to be ideal for use with ATM machines, and dial-in networks like AOL and Prodigy also employed it as well. Given that track record, it is not surprising the X.25 came to be adopted by many cellular networks.

As previously noted, cellular carriers have switching offices that are referred to (alternatively) as "switches," Mobil Telephone Switching Offices (MTSOs) or Mobile Switching Centers (MSCs). These switches have to communicate with other switches and databases within a network, and for those internal messages X.25 was superb. But it was a different matter when a cellular subscriber was roaming on another network, and that's where X.25 was inadequate.

In order to connect with another network, the previously described Signal Transfer Point (STP) would function as a gateway to access databases in other telecom networks. Unfortunately, it was the very architecture that made X.25 made it ideal for financial institutions also made it unusable outside of its own network. Bear in mind that X.25 was developed prior to SS7, and it was economical. SS7, on the other hand, arrived later and was not by any means inexpensive. But despite the cost, by the 1980s telephony was becoming much more reliant on databases. In addition, SS7 had a crucial advantage: i.e., it could establish a signal communication without establishing a point-to-point connection. Those capabilities favored the deployment of SS7, and that's what most telecoms did.

To really appreciate the sea change that SS7 and its database capabilities ushered in, one only has to look at the customer experience. As recently as the 1990s (and sometimes later), most cellphone users had a geographically limited service. Due to the size limits and a propensity to travel, it would not be uncommon for a subscriber to travel outside his or her service area. When someone would call a number that had roamed outside the service area, a recording would typically announced that the destination number was either unavailable or outside the service area. In some cases, a subscriber would actually use a second telephone number to enable calls to go through when he/she was outside the home service area and homing off a different network. How times have changed!

In the second decade of the twenty-first century, cellular networks are ubiquitous. Just consider how much cellular networks have grown. At the end of that 1996, there were 44.0 million wireless subscriber connections within the United States. Five years later, the number had increased to 128.4 million and, in December 2006 – a decade after the new telecommunications law was passed – the number of wireless connections reached 233.0 million. By this time the number of mobile device users had exceeded the number of landline phones, with three such connections for every four Americans. Five years later, at the end of 2011, another 98 million subscribers were added, bring the total number of wireless subscriber connections to 331.6 million.[10] Consumers have been voting for mobility, often completely forsaking any wireline home service. This growth would not have been possible without SS7. But data on the growth of cellular networks doesn't tell the entire story.

Another factor that the performance of telecommunication networks – and the customer experience – is complexity. Complexity applies both to the network architecture and the physical and software components that comprise the elements of the network. As cellular networks evolve, the migration from 2G/3G[11] to 4G/LTE[12] and 4G/VoLTE[13] introduces both inherent complexities, and others that relate to migration itself. In particular, the integration of the TCP/IP environment, smartphones and what are often referred to as Over-the-Top (OTT), or value-added services,[14] present special challenges, not the least of which affect signaling. Just the move from legacy 2G to 3G networks greatly increased the number of signals; with Internet-based services and more complex smartphones, the growth in signal traffic has been exponential.

In addition, OTT services make the established phone networks less important to customers. OTT services transfer both customer loyalty and revenue to the OTT service providers. The dilution of voice and text messaging (SMS) traffic affects the carrier's revenue models at a time when they have collectively been spending many tens of billions of dollars for network upgrades in their SS7/SIGTRAN environment. Because of the prior (and very large investments in 2G/3G infrastructure, it is understandable that carriers want to move with some deliberation to an IP-based architecture.

The carriers want to retain customer loyalty and revenue in the Internet-based world, yet they find themselves with customers who use Skype, Wi-Fi WhatsApp or Viber. It's a global problem, too. South Korea's telecoms took a big financial hit when smartphone users in that country started to use KakaoTalk instead of the carrier's own text-messaging services. But despite the regularity of market-based changes that affect the customer experience, subscribers are often aware of unaware of the technological and economic factors that deliver these benefits. Getting more information to subscribers, especially concerning such very basic things as the vagaries their radio connections, remains an unmet challenge.

• • •

With the arrival of twenty-first century networks, other entities become involved with the delivery of features. One step forward toward the convergence of voice and data delivery was the development of IP Multimedia Subsystems (IMS).[15] Somewhat like a symphony orchestra, open-standard IMS provides an integrated telephony solution that the earlier Intelligent Network (IN) concept failed to realize. IMS can work on wireline and cellular networks as well as the Internet, but it is the roaming capability that cellular networks provide that enables IMS to fully blossom.

With IMS, the Call Session Control Function (CSCF)[16] becomes a node for signal routing regardless of what network the subscriber is using. CSCF uses the Session Initiation Protocol (SIP), with subscriber information being provided from the Home Subscriber Service (HSS). HSS provides the database function that enables authentication of the user and verification that a particular service is

109

authorized. You may notice the similarity of HSS to the legacy AAA servers that we discussed earlier, although legacy AAA uses RADIUS and IMS uses the more secure DIAMETER protocol to support HSS. With IMS, SIP application servers can manage the content that is being provided to the user.

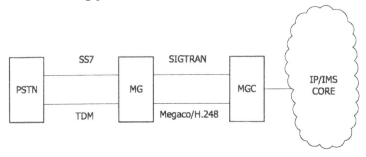

Relationship between a Public Switched Telephone Network (PSTN), Media Gateway (MG) and related Media Gateway Controller (MGC), and the IP Multimedia Subsystem (IMS).

In the convergence that IMS fosters, SIP becomes the key cross-platform signaling protocol. Because IMS operates as a subsystem (albeit a pervasive one), SIP can provide its signaling function with all types of content providers, while the previously discussed ISUP operates in the control plane. However, SS7 is still functional with the wireline and cellular carriers; in the overall operational scheme, it's just pushed farther into the background. That's because changing a telecommunications network, especially for the larger carriers, is an enormous, multi-year job. In the legacy networks, SS7 continues to function with ISUP. However, once a network (or portion thereof) migrates to IP, ISUP is replaced by SIP, which supports voice and media. In addition, RADIUS is replaced by DIAMETER, which also replaces the MAP for accessing the Home Subscriber Service (HSS). H.248 is the preferred protocol for the Media Gateway Controller (MGC); it connects the legacy phone company's Time Division Multiplexing (TDM)[17] infrastructure with the IP networks. Because of all this, smartphones are really smart and cellular users have a device that is more than just a telephone. Our lives are much different as a result of this.

By the second decade of the twenty-first century, and despite the huge leaps in technology, public awareness of telephony and the convergence of technologies remains deficient. That makes additional problems for the telecom carriers, which have their own set of challenges. With hundreds of millions of subscribers, carriers have eliminated operators but replaced them with call centers for customer service and tech support functions. And in the post-operator world in which people stay connected, those call centers are busy.

To get a flavor of what cellular carriers deal with during customer interactions, consider these rather typical scenarios: a voice telephone call from Flagstaff, Arizona to Kokomo, Indiana fails to process correctly and generates a recorded error message; text messages from Cincinnati, Ohio fail to reach the destination number in Mindanao (in the Philippines); a picture message from an iPhone in Port Arthur, Texas fails to download onto a Motorola handset in Seattle, Washington; a service outage that includes failing 911 emergency calls develops in Spencerport, NY, and Blackberry Internet Service (BIS) email that originates from different services fails to sync to a recently activated Blackberry in Nashville, Tennessee. Almost all of these problems would not have existed with Plain Old Telephone Service (POTS).

Achieving high levels of customer satisfaction in the twenty-first century will involve better customer education, and that has to begin with fundamental knowledge of both current technologies and end user devices. Understanding the RF limitations of low-powered cellphones is one of the fundamentals, especially when the user is indoors or in any environment with low to nil RSSI[18] values. Basic handset operation is important, and that includes being about to send and receive text messages (SMS), picture/video messages (MMS) and email. All of this goes on the "need to know" list.

Another area of general awareness concerns device architecture. Increasingly, handsets are being affected by problems that derive from software and firmware. Software includes a cellphone's operating system and applications software, the latter being an especially common cause of functionality problems. Firmware is a term that has some ambiguity. As commonly used, it applies to a fixed control or operating system that is stored in the ROM; it usually comes from the original equipment manufacturer (OEM). Firmware updates can often be downloaded over-the-air (OTA, or FOTA for firmware-over-the-air), and "flashed" into the handset's ROM. It is important to note that this is of a fixed nature and separate from the phone's regular storage. The nomenclature is indicative how closely firmware is associated with the hardware.

Learning more about handsets, wireless modems and basic characteristics of cellular networks is important, but consumers need to appreciate another matter. The economic factors and financial risks of modern telephony are significant, and have outcomes that affect all consumers. Prior to 1984, telephone systems basically operated as regulated monopolies. The financial risk was not significant in that the regulatory scheme allowed for the recovery of most costs. That all changed in a competitive marketplace, and the list of carriers that failed or merged is telling. Moreover, the investment in the build out of cellular networks, 4G technologies such as LTE and the emergence of IMS cost the telecoms many tens of billions of dollars in any given year.

Cellular carriers have other costs that wireline carriers don't have, one of them being the purchase of handsets for resale to subscribers. Today a high percentage of these handsets are smartphones, many of which are sold at a loss in return for the customer's subscription renewal. In addition, many carriers suffer financial losses while dealing with handset and replacement issues. SS7 cannot ameliorate these issues, but in other ways it can reduce costs to the carrier and the customer. We've already mentioned least-cost routing (LCR), but fraud detection and data collection for marketing are other examples of how SS7 helps networks lower their costs.

Contrary to what many consumers believe, higher operating costs affect the consumer because they affect pricing decisions. SS7 helps networks detect fraud because it can quickly and easily produce call detail records (CDRs). This is not much different from call data that is used in the creation of network trouble tickets, except that fraud can impose significant costs if left unchecked. In the area of marketing, networks mine data to evaluate how customers use the network. Unlike sales, marketing is oriented towards customer needs, which relates to demand for particular products and services. This is turn affects decisions on pricing, advertising and promotions, and how offered services are structured. The use of information that is derived from signaling data is a far cry from what was possible with in-band or out-of-band signaling!

One thing that consumers also need is peace of mind. Free markets can be somewhat disorderly, as evidenced by the changed landscape of telecom service providers. In general, consumers have a wide range of end-user products available (e.g., basic cellphones, smartphones and modems), calling plans and services. Even such now routine items as ringback tones and visual voicemail were not common until the early years of the twenty-first century. Despite the progress, there is often a public perception that the surviving (and generally large) wireline and cellular carriers are not sensitive to public needs. The excerpt of FCC data at the beginning of Section Five provides evidence of these concerns, as do actual calls into national call centers of the carriers.

Even with the proliferation of 4G networks with LTE technology, it is common for cellular service subscribers to question poor radio connections. Complaints of poor radio signals indoors, or in areas when RSSI values are low, often result from a lack of consumer knowledge. In cases where a subscriber purchases a smartphone that has recurring technical issues, there is too often a belief that the cellular network is responsible. The successful integration of hardware and software, especially with the proliferation of applications and app providers, creates a new degree of complexity for handsets. Issues with handsets often get directed to the cellular network, in part because the service provider sold the device during a contract renewal. Unfortunately, greater device complexity introduces reliability issues, which customers must be made aware of.

Another area of disconnect between networks and their customers pertains to the manner in which service issues are typically resolved. In the majority of cases, customers will speak over the phone with a call center representative for both device and non-device related service issues. Typically, the person at the call center is a customer service representative with a fairly broad portfolio of skills. Technical issues that cannot be resolved at the customer service level are then escalated to technical support. Tech support reps have a variety of tools to analyze device and network issues, and to determine exactly what type of issue is present.

Tech support issues that involve the network are typically evaluated in a number of ways, including details of voice and data connections. Once again, SS7 yields an enormous advantage by producing data about each and every call that would not be available from the various switches. Details such as call condition indicator

(CCI) values, termination codes (TC), error codes and seizures (i.e., the number of seconds that the connect lasted) are all available to tech support reps. Tech support reps typically have special tools to do a quick dropped call analysis for voice calls, and can check such important metrics as the signal-to-noise ratio (SNR) on data connections. Unresolved network-related issues often result in the creation of a trouble ticket.

On the matter of public safety, issues involving call failures to the '911' emergency number immediately receive special handling and a 911-trouble ticket. Unknown to the general public, network executives with oversight responsibility for network operations monitor the status of their network around the clock. That degree of oversight enables resources to be directed to major problem areas, as when a hurricane or some other severe weather impacts a region.

Even with all these safeguards, the significance of a major service outage is not always immediately apparent. Consider a service outage that suddenly occurs in a particular town. Calls come into the call centers and get routed to tech support, and trouble tickets are opened. But trouble tickets are compartmentalized. Once they are sent to the network repair agency, each ticket is classified according to the type of underlying problem. If trouble tickets for the same problem are alternatively classified under the categories 'low signal,' 'no signal where previously present,' 'unable to send,' 'unable to receive' and 'dropped call,' then the repair agency may – at least for a time – not realize that they have a one significant outage. Rather, they may see a number of completely dissimilar problems showing up. And that can happen, especially if customers alternatively describe the same outage as a problem with dropped calls, an inability to make outbound calls, a failure to receive incoming calls, or a low signal. Sometimes it is a person in tech support who, seeing different types of tickets being opened in the same area, finally connects the dots and sounds the alarm for a major outage.

SS7 has made the cadre of tech support, network repair agency and cell site technicians far more capable and responsive than would have otherwise been possible. So signaling has become more that signals, an outcome that flows from Dr. Claude Shannon's information revolution in communications. Even with the convergence of technologies, SS7 remains a sophisticated data transfer system, operating in real time, and making crucial information about calls available to those who need it.

To the above thoughts it should be noted that the overwhelming majority of customer-facing reps in customer service and tech support very much enjoy helping people. These front-line workers do their best to solve myriad handset problems, investigate peripheral issues within their scope of support, and open trouble tickets for '911' failures and network service outages. It's all done in a very demanding, fast-paced environment. No system is perfect, but the knowledge, skills and experience of call center and network personnel often lead to faster service restorations. That's something that upset customers ought to remember when they speak to someone at a network call center.

Section Five Footnotes

1   Note: Network engineers take a pretty sophisticated view of cell tower siting, as they understand that user population, terrain and other factors that affect cellular connections. See also U.S. Patent No. 4,144,411, entitled 'Cellular radiotelephone system structured for flexible use of different cell sizes,' which was filed on September 22, 1976 by Richard H. Freakiel of Bell Telephone Laboratories. The patent was issued on March 13, 1979. Source: USPTO.

2   See U.S. Patent 6,539,227, entitled 'Methods and Systems For Controlling Hard and Soft Handoffs in Radio Communications Systems,' filed by Ulrich Jetzek, et al on Dec 17, 1999, and issued on March 25, 2003. Retrieved on November 6, 2012 from:
    http://www.google.com/patents/US6539227?printsec=abstract#v=onepage&q&f=false

3   Note: ARPANET is the acronym for the former Advanced Research Projects Agency network. A forerunner of the Internet, ARPANET was the first operational packet switched network and was in service from 1969-1989. See 'Brief History of the Internet,' copyright © 2012 The Internet Society, and retrieved on November 6, 2012 from:

www.internetsociety.org/what-internet/history-internet/brief-history-internet.

4   Note: TCP is the acronym for Transmission Control Protocol, and IP is the acronym for Internet protocol. Known formally as the Internet Protocol Suite, it was developed in 1974. See: 'A Protocol for Packet Network Intercommunication,' by Vinton G. Cerf and Robert E. Kahn, IEEE *Transactions on Communications* Vol-Com 22 (5), May, 1974: 637-648, copyright © 1974 IEEE, all rights reserved.

5   Note: The NSFNET was operational from 1985-95. Source: National Science Foundation (NSF), retrieved on November 6, 2012 from:
    http://www.nsfnet-legacy.org.

6   See *Signaling System 7* (Fifth Edition) by Travis Russell, copyright © 2006 by The McGraw-Hill Companies, p. 111 on packet switching.

7   Note: Science and Engineering Research Council.

8   Note: PADS provide multiple path asynchronous data connectivity to an X.25 network. See ITU-T Recommendations X.3, X.28 and X.29.

9   Note: Telenet, founded in 1974, was also the first serve company to make packet switching network services available to the general public. It was acquired by GTE in 1979.

10 Source: '50 Wireless Quick Facts,' published online by CTIA, and retrieved on November 6, 2012 from: http://www.ctia.org/media/publications.

11 Note: 2G is the acronym for second-generation cellular network technology. 2G, which was introduced in 1991, is a digital technology, and replaced the predecessor analog technology. 2G uses either TDMA (Time Division Multiple Access) or CDMA (Code Division Multiple Access) multiplexing. 3G is the acronym for third-generation cellular network technology, and is based on the IMT-2000 standard of the ITU.

12 Note: 4G is the acronym for fourth generation cellular network technology. LTE is the acronym for Long Term Evolution, a particular (and favored) type of fourth generation technology.

13 Note: 4G/VoLTE refers to a 4G/LTE network where both voice and data are carried by LTE. The LTE standard was developed by 3GPP. Some networks have offered technologies that were touted as "4G" that not not comply with the specifications of ITU-R in its IMT-Advanced standard.

14 Note: OTT (Over-the-Top), or value-added services, are applications (apps) and other services that are neither developed nor branded by the telecommunications carrier; they are merely transported by the carrier. These technically non-conforming technologies include WiMAX, HSPA+ and LTE. After several carriers publically advertised WiMAX. HSPA+ and LTE as 4G technologies, ITU decided to include them in a generic 4G nomenclature, while referring to those technologies that actually meet all the IMT-Advanced specifications as "True LTE." See press release from ITU-R entitled 'ITU-R Confers IMT-Advanced (4G) Status to 3GPP LTE,' dated October, 2010, and retrieved on November 6, 2012 from: http://www.3gpp.org/ITU-R-Confers-IMT-Advanced-4G.

15 Note: IMS is a Next Generation Network (NGN) standard that uses VoIP. IMS is designed to provide networks with more control over content that their networks provide. However, the basic LTE does not support circuit switched voice traffic, so networks that handle voice calls using CDMA2000, GSM and UMTS technologies will have to adopt either VoLTE, Circuit Switched Fallback (CSFB) or Simultaneous Voice and LTE (SVLTE). See the 3GPP Specification Detail provided in 'IP Multimedia Subsystem (IMS); Stage 2,' retrieved on November 6, 2012 from: http://www.3gpp.org/ftp/Specs/html-info/23228.htm.

16 See *Signaling System 7* (Fifth Edition) by Travis Russell, copyright © 2006 by The
McGraw-Hill Companies, p. 20 on Call Session Control Function (CSCF) general description, and p. 665-666 on CSCF proxy, interrogation and serving functions for IMS.

117

17 Note: Time-Division Multiplexing (TDM) is a methodology in which multiple bit streams (signals) are transported in subchannels within a particular communications channel. TDM is an alternative to packet-mode transport. See *Signaling System 7* (Fifth Edition) by Travis Russell, copyright © 2006 by The McGraw-Hill Companies, p. 61 on call setup and tear down in TDM in circuit switched networks, p. 105 on SS7 in TDM circuit switched networks, p. 110 on BISUP not utilizing TDM circuit codes, p. 112-113 on TDM reliance on the MTP portion of the SS7 protocol stack for routing, management link management, and p. 131 on the MTP portion of the SS7 protocol stack.

18 Note: RSSI is an acronym for Received Radio Strength Indication, and is a measurement of the power available of a received radio signal. On a scale to (2.g.) 100, a higher number indicated a stronger signal. Units are arbitrary, and the measurement is made of the unamplified signal that arrives at the handset antenna. As used in this text, DSSI refers to the IEEE 802.11 standards for the wireless environment.

Epilogue

When you're backed up in that situation, when you get a
40-yard gain, that changes your play calling.

- NY Giants Quarterback Eli Manning, commenting
  on the 38-yard pass to wide receiver Mario
  Manningham that set up the game-winning drive
  in Super Bowl XLVI.

By getting more from the spectrum that we already have, we
can get 10 times higher data speeds for our wireless
networks, and we can do it all without asking for additional
spectrum.

- Dr. Dina Katabi, Professor of Electrical and Computer
  Science Engineering at the Massachusetts Institute of
  Technology and Co-Director of the MIT Center for
  Wireless Networks and Mobile Computing, in an
  October 11, 2012 article in MITnews entitled:
  'Engineering MIT's CSAIL launches new center to
  tackle the future of wireless and mobile technologies.'
  Copyright © 2012 MIT News, all rights reserved.

Left end Justin Tuck led the charge, as the New York Giants'
defensive line pushed the New England Patriots back into the end
zone. Patriots' quarterback Tom Brady was able to get off a pass,
with the football sailing down to the fifty-yard line – but far away
from any receivers. NFL referee John Parry ruled that the pass was
an intentional grounding, so the first score in the game was a 2-point
safety against New England. It was February 5, 2012, and Super
Bowl XLVI was underway at Lucas Oil Stadium in Indianapolis.

Super Bowl XLVI, which the Giants won by a score of 21-17, was
a thriller; the game was seen by 111 million television viewers and
68,658 attendees. Overall, team stats showed a remarkable
similarity. Giants' quarterback Eli Manning passed for 296 yards and

was the game's Most Valuable Player. Giants' running back Ahmad Bradshaw rushed for 72 yards and one touchdown, while his wide receiver teammate Hakeem Hicks made 10 receptions and gained 109 yards. Patriots' quarterback Tom Brady passed for 276 yards, while running back BenJarvus Green-Ellis rushed for 44 yards in 10 carries. Patriots' tight end Aaron Hernandez was also productive, receiving 8 passes and gaining 67 yards.

Even with all that action, the biggest play of the game didn't come until the end of the fourth quarter. With 57 seconds left on the game clock, Bradshaw made a highly unorthodox 6-yard touchdown run that delivered the Giants a come from behind victory.[1] Yet despite the excitement of the game, some of the biggest plays were being quietly made off the field by Verizon Wireless, AT&T and Sprint Nextel.

Well in advance of Super Bowl XLVI, the National Football League recognized that capturing the maximum fan interest had to involve more than new stadiums. Interactive media that gave ticketholders a way to connect with family members and friends would be a crucial to building a stronger customer base. That effort was important, since in recent years the NFL had seen declining ticket sales that new stadiums alone would not ameliorate. In 2010, the NFL and team owners began to implement a plan to offer the RedZone Channel in 32 stadiums. And in preparation for the championship game, Lucas Oil Stadium (home of the Indianapolis Colts) was equipped with a WiFi network and a 500 antenna Distributed Antenna System (DAS) by Corning MobileAccess. Lucas Oil Field was the fifth NFL stadium to be so equipped, and followed similar practices at Olympic games and other major events.[2]

The DAS that was installed in Lucas Oil Field proved to be highly effective, but the plan for Super Bowl coverage extended far beyond the periphery of the stadium. The area that included Indianapolis International Airport, Indiana Convention Center, JW Marriott Indianapolis and seven additional hotels all we seamlessly provided wireless service. For the game day, Verizon Wireless, AT&T and Sprint Nextel each set up temporary network facilities to augment their existing infrastructure. Super Bowl XLVI was televised by NBC, streamed online by NBC.com and available to cellphones through the Verizon Wireless NFL Mobile app. The online stream would be only a small percentage of the television viewership, but there would be a different set of advertisers. The marketing scheme was going to boost fan support by working on the margins.

Looking behind the scenes, the cellular networks' preparations as the game day approached were robust. Perhaps the most visible parts involved a number of small Cell On Wheels (COW) trailers and Cell On Light Truck (COLT) facilities. In addition to its COWs and COLTs, Verizon Wireless had nine antennas in their own DAS outside the stadium, and provided both 3G and 4G-LTE data service. AT&T had a similar arrangement, including its WiFi Hotzone in the downtown area. Sprint Nextel had two COWs each at Lucas Oil Stadium and the practice field at the University of Indianapolis; the network also upgraded CDMA and iDEN cell sites in the area.[3] All of the cellular networks performed well before, during and after the game.

The NFL was also aware of other avenues for drawing fan interest. One of them – Fantasy Football – had existed in various forms for decades, yet it wasn't until the late 1990s that the popularity of Fantasy leagues began to grow rapidly. However, at the time of this writing, it is the leading marketing tool of the NFL. Based on the NFL experience, it is clear that Fantasy Football provides a reality check for other businesses that have yet to discover the full benefits of cross-channel marketing. By 2012, the number of Fantasy Football participants (in all leagues) was approaching 20 million. It is easy to see why the future of telephony involves a convergence of IP-based technologies and platforms, many of which are married to upgraded legacy infrastructures.

2012 was also the year of the London Summer Olympics. After seven years of extensive preparations, the games began on July 27th at Olympic Park in the Stratford section of East London. Broadcast rights for the Olympics were highly prized. The BBC held the home nation rights in the United Kingdom, while in the United States NBC acquired the rights for a premium price of $1.18 billion. The cable networks ESPN and Eurosport also bought a piece of the action, while NBC partnered with YouTube to provide a livestream on the Web.

Perhaps even more interesting than broadcast rights were the number of mobile applications ("apps") associated with the 2012 Olympics. The Olympics began a little more than two years after

Apple's iPad first went on sale. The iPad and iPhone both operated with Apple's proprietary iOS operating system, and both devices were popular with app developers. A number of competing devices used Google's Android operating system, an open source mobile platform that was developed using the Linux kernel. Android complied with the Open Handset Alliance (OHA) mandates, so apps for devices that ran on Android were plentiful. Android version 4.1 ("Jelly Bean") was released just two weeks before the Olympics began. So during the summer of 2012, handset and tablet users were able to view the Olympics with apps such as *NBC Olympics Live Extra, Join In, London 2012 Official Mobile Game, London 2012 Results* – and many more.

The juxtaposition of apps and the mutual trends of Internet use and social networking produced a global synergy; there were new social protocols in communication that were as unique as the World Wide Web itself. Facebook, the world's leading social website, became a publically traded company in May 2012. Four months later, the social network had over one billion active users, double the July 2010 level. And less than one year after that, the site had over one trillion page views within a one-month period.

Six-year old Twitter reached the half-billion active user mark at roughly the same time that Facebook reached the one billion user mark, and became one of the ten most visited websites in the world. Flickr, the image and video hosting site that Yahoo! purchased in 2005, was well liked for its groups, public and private storage of images, and geotagging. And Skype, a VoIP service that Microsoft purchased in 2011, was experiencing phenomenal growth. Just days before the 2012 London Olympics began, Microsoft confirmed the trend: Skype had provided of 115 billion minutes of calls during the three-month period that ended in June. That usage was fifty-percent higher than the traffic volume for the previous three months.

Clearly, consumers around the globe were accepting social networking as part of their daily lives. Facebook, Google-Plus, Twitter, YouTube, Flickr and other services had, within just a number of years, become part of the modern world's social fabric. Along with that, individuals were demonstrating a willingness to relinquish privacy for a communal embrace, but not without some apprehension. There was a basis for some concern. In an August 2012 report entitled 'Understanding What They Do With What

They Know,' Worcester Polytechnic Institute Professors Craig E. Wills and graduate student Can Tatar noted:

> *In an initial study of ad networks and a focused study of the Google ad network, we found many contextual, behavioral and location-based ads along with combinations of these types of ads. We also observed profile based ads. Most behavioral ads were shown as categories in the Ad Preference Manager (APM) of the ad network, but we found unexpected cases where the interests were not visible in the APM. We also fund unexpected behavior for the Google ad network in that non-contextual ads were shown related to induced sensitive topics regarding sexual orientation, health and financial matters.*
>
> *In a smaller study of Facebook, we did not find clear evidence that a user's browsing behavior on non-Facebook site influences the ads shown to the consumer on Facebook, but we did observe such influence when the Facebook Like button is used to express interest in content. We did observe Facebook ads appearing to target users for sensitive interests with some ads even asserting such sensitive information, which appears to be a violation of Facebook's stated policy.[4]*

There was a segment of the American public that feared privacy invasions by law enforcement agencies, even if the actions were far less intrusive. This became evident in October 2012, when United States Magistrate Judge Brian L. Owsley (in the Southern District of Texas) made a preliminary ruling against the use of "stingrays" and "cell tower dumps" without a search warrant. In combating domestic terrorists and organized crime, federal law enforcement agencies were reportedly making roughly 1.3 million requests per year on subscriber activity. While the need to locate missing persons and take other emergency actions was generally acknowledged, the chorus of concerns about the high number of requests grew increasingly louder. In particular, the salient legal question about the need for search warrants was being raised in amicus briefs by Fourth Amendment and privacy advocates. Not surprisingly, federal law enforcement officials took opposing views, and often with very good reasons.

Aside from law enforcement, privacy concerns evolved from the ubiquitous use of cameras at traffic lights, workplace locations and a litany of public places. Citizens were increasingly aware of twenty-first century intrusiveness, but the level of concern remained uneven. All of the above intrusions involve digital data, all of which can be transported via telephony or over the Internet. Most Americans seemed to have a deep ambivalence about privacy, with no consensus about where the boundaries should be. Many of those concerns were addressed again in the 34th International Conference of Data Protection and Privacy Commissioners at Punta del Este, Uruguay (October 22-24, 2012). In time, the public will find those answers. Meanwhile, life in America went on.

And despite the anemic macroeconomy, life was good. Cellphones had become more than mobile telephones; they had become small screen media centers. Teenagers and adults of all ages were listening to Pandora and Slacker Radio on their iPhones and Droids. Owners of Kindle, Nook and other ereaders could download bestsellers like Gillian Flynn's *Gone Girl*, E. L. James *Fifty Shades of Grey*, or Tom Clancy's *Threat Vector*. Visitors to New York City could utilize apps such as NYC Way, Coovents or iParks NY. Sports teams, restaurants, orchestras and wineries had apps, and travelers could get GPS navigations services through their phones. Stock prices, market news, financial transactions and weather information are all available online, and could also be delivered to a cellphone, modem or tablet.

The plethora of apps and services that existed in the marketplace proved to be a mixed blessing for the carriers. Branded services had been an important revenue component for the cellular networks, but the networks no longer had a lock on that revenue. Over the Top (OTT) providers of content have now usurped a considerable amount of marketing and economic power from telecom carriers; with evolving LTE networks and IP-based architecture that shift in loyalty may be permanent. Perhaps just as significant are how the new trends in web-based offerings will affect the networks that deliver the rich content to consumers. For years network executives have been watching the growth of data service on legacy 2G/3G networks. Now the watching is over; the future has arrived.

One manifestation of the increased demand on networks is the increased number of "signal storms." Signal storms are basically function failures that occur when the servers that service a network's signaling system get overwhelmed to the point that the network can't function One example is the June, 2011 network outage that affected the Norwegian cellular carrier Telenor. Telenor's outage began after a software update for the carrier's IP services. However, the carrier soon found that on its legacy phone network signaling and database servers were being overwhelmed by an extremely high volume of messages. The result was that during the Pentecost holiday weekend, some three millions subscribers were without service during an 18-hour period.

Other carriers have also experienced signal storms and related issues. In April 2011, Verizon Wireless suffered a daylong outage on its 4G/LTE network. The outage began simple enough; the root cause was reported to be a software issue on the IP Multimedia Subsystem (IMS). Verizon, which was reportedly spending over $6 billion/year on its network, had not been skimping. Verizon Wireless's 4G/LTE network relied on numerous vendors for design, equipment and support, and the 4G/LTE architecture was intricate. Unfortunately, the problem migrated over to the legacy 3G network, even though it only affected 4G subscribers. That portion of the problem was due to the fact that when 4G handsets that roamed into 3G areas of Verizon's service area, they did not utilize the 3G high-rate packet data (HRPD) functionality of the 3G network. Instead, Verizon's 4G subscribers stayed on the 4G IMS core. As a result, 4G smartphones lost data capabilities while older 3G handsets functioned normally.

So the great advantages of 4G/LTE networks came with complexity, even though Verizon Wireless did not initially utilize Voice-Over-LTE (VoLTE). In the case of Verizon Wireless, the voice portion of LTE wasn't even planned for commissioning until roughly 2013. Perhaps most significantly, the wonders of high-speed downloads on the 4G technology required vastly more signals than did the 2G/3G network with SS7. Given the different methodology and the enormous increases in web-based data usage, networks were learning that the transition to 4G/LTE would not be trouble free. But besides far higher upload and download speeds, the new generation of telephony came with numerous behind the scene advantages.

One of the big advantages with the newer 4G/LTE networks is their use of the DIAMETER protocol for AAA functions instead of the obsolete RADIUS. In addition to having significant security advantages, DIAMETER is also well suited for signaling in an environment where call setup and teardown are but one of the signaling imperatives. In fact, as 3GPP expands its role in 4G/LTE networks, DIAMETER replaces TAP and CAP protocols in billing functions, and it also replaces the MAP protocol in cellular networks.

Along with those pluses, however, is a big minus: i.e., with DIAMETER and a more intricate accounting and authentication environment, the huge increase in AAA server demands, added to the huge increase in smartphone users and OTT applications, all combine to generate extremely high levels of signaling traffic. And as if that weren't enough of a challenge, spikes in that traffic can render a network vulnerable to the point where outages occur.

Other challenges are also unfolding. As of 2012, carriers that have inaugurated 4G/LTE service in the United States had not transitioned to VoIP; they still relied on legacy 2G/3G infrastructure and methodologies. Voice-over-LTE (VoLTE) is the next step in the migration, and that will be a multi year process. While this is going on, networks will be facing an increase of machine-to-machine (M2M) communications. M2M doesn't just involve computers talking to production machinery on remove assembly lines. With M2M, fleet owners and even small companies can track the position of vehicles and packages. In industrial settings, when M2M is used to remotely control machine operations, additional communications may be used for quality control and the management of facility electrical systems. In medicine, implanted medical devices can be remotely monitored, and public utilities can remotely take meter readings and send the data to automated billing systems. On the individual level, cellular subscribers will be able to control the lighting and temperature of their home from anywhere in the country, and from much of the civilized world.

All of these demands will require even more sophisticated management of signaling loads, especially as 4G/LTE becomes more widespread. There will have to be better management of available bandwidth, and improved techniques for handoffs as handsets roam from on different 4G/LTE networks, or from a 4G network to a 2G/3G network. The number of signals that smartphones generate will also have to be managed, especially when a handset is activated. Activation of an iPhone, for example, requires several times as many signals as predecessor smartphones.

Operating quietly in the background of this new telecommunications world are the ubiquitous 2G/3G networks. And just like the wheel, a lot of tried and proven technology plays an important role. A visit to a MTSO will reveal that a considerable amount of direct current is used in the electronic world, along with softswitches, gateways and routers. As a result switching offices have backup generators and very large battery banks (with very large protection systems) that can be used as emergency power sources. None of this is visible to the public, but those expensive assets are there – and they are extremely reliable.

People also matter, and people that the public seldom sees have a lot to do with the success of SS7 and the legacy 2G/3G networks the form the backbone of our telecommunications network. Every major telephone company – cellular or wireline – has senior executives who monitor network operations around the clock. Network operations teams include system performance and network engineers, switch and cell site technicians, and those groups that process and monitor trouble tickets. These groups provide 24/7 coverage every day of the year, holidays included. How well these groups perform is often revealed in the aftermath of severe weather and natural disasters. The most telling example in recent years was Hurricane Katrina, which came ashore over the coasts of Mississippi and Louisiana on August 28, 2005.

"The storm incubated very, very rapidly and intensified very, very rapidly to a very, very strong hurricane," noted Dr. Jeffrey Halverson, professor of meteorology at the University of Maryland (NASA film 'In Katrina's Wake'). "And you couldn't really find anywhere [sic] you could escape from this thing." [5]

The National Oceanic and Atmospheric Administration (NOAA) rates Katrina as the deadliest storm to ever strike the United States, with roughly 1,863 deaths being attributed to it. Most significantly, failures of the levee system that protects New Orleans contributed to major flooding following the storm surge, but the unusually large size of the hurricane resulted in major damage as the diminishing storm roared northward across Louisiana and Mississippi. A senior official in the Defense Department noted that "the magnitude of the storm was such that the local communications system wasn't simply degraded; it was, at least for a period of time, destroyed." No fewer than 38 Emergency 911 centers in Mississippi and Louisiana went down, along with 100 radio stations, much of the wireline telephone infrastructure; nearly 2,000 cell towers were rendered inoperative (at least for a time) the geographic area that lost communications was roughly 90,000 square miles, or about the size of Great Britain.[6]

Hurricane Katrina revealed that some carriers were better prepared than others. In general, the cell towers in Mississippi and Louisiana withstood the high winds, although numerous antennas were blown out of alignment. Base station flooding and fuel exhaustion for backup generations proved to be the main problems, although equipment issues contributed to some delays. But overall cellular networks responded quickly, and more than a few workers in tech support noted with pride the rate at which their engineers and technicians restored damaged facilities to service.

In the days that followed, residents of Franklin, Madison and Carroll Counties in Mississippi started making calls as power to base stations was restored and damaged antennas were fixed. Calls to and from residents of New Orleans, Lafayette and New Iberia, Louisiana started to process normally when power to their towers came back. But in the background, one important part of the restoration remained unnoticed by the public. As the crippled infrastructure was restored, it was SS7 that began routing tens of millions of calls to reconnect the devastated region and its people to worried relatives and friends. For all those who designed, built, commissioned, monitored and maintained SS7 – the world's greatest civilian signaling system – it was a quiet but proud legacy.

Epilogue Footnotes

1   See http://www.nfl.com/superbowl/46

2   See Corning Cable Systems News Release entitled 'Corning MobileAccess Brings Wall-to-Wall Wireless Coverage to Indianapolis for Super Bowl XLVI and Beyond'. January 31, 2012. Retrieved from:
    http://www.corning.com/cablesystems/nafta/en/news_events/news_releases/2012/2012013001.aspx.

3   See 'Super Bowl Stadium AT&T GalaxyTabs, VZW COWS & Free Wi-Fis, Sprint & Ready for Super Wireless' by Lynn Walford, Jan 23, 2012. Retrieved from:

http://wirelessandmobilenews.com/2012/01/super-bowl-stadium-cows-verizon-4g-lte-tailgating.html.

4   See Abstract of report entitled 'Understanding What They Do With What They Know' by Craig Willis and Can Tatar, WPI-CS-TR-12-03, Computer Science Technical Report Series, Computer Science Dept., Worcester Polytechnic Institute, August 2012. Abstract available (10-25-2012) at: http://www.cs.wpi.edu/~cew/papers/tr1203.pdf.   Retrieved from:
http://web.cs.wpi.edu/~cew/papers/wpes12.pdf.

5   See 'In Katrina's Wake' produced by NASA at NASA.gov (2007). Retrieved from:
Hurricane_Katrina_(short_film_by_NASA).gov
(Ogg multilplexed audio/video file, Theora/Vorbis).

6   See 'Hurricane Katrina: Communications & Infrastructure Impacts' by Dr. Robert Miller, Senior Research Professor, National Defense University, included in *Threats At Our Threshold: Homeland Defense and Homeland Security in the New Century*, (A Compilation of the Proceedings of the First Annual Homeland Defense and Homeland Security Conference [Sponsored by Eisenhower National Security Series; Executive Agent: United States Army War College, Carlisle Barracks, PA]), 2007, Edited by Bert B. Tussing, p. 193-4. Retrieved from:
www.gwumc.edu/hspi/policy/CHDSA2006.pdf.

Glossary

1ESS: No. 1 Electronic Switching System
1XB: No. 1 Crossbar Switch
3G: 3rd generation of cellular technology
3GPP: 3rd Generation Partnership Project
4G: 4th generation of cellular technology
4XB: No. 4 Crossbar (Tandem) Switch
5XB: No. 5 Crossbar Switch

AAA (server): authentication, authorization & accounting (server)
a-c: alternating electrical current
AAR: automatic alternate routing
AEA: Alexander Graham Bell's Aerial Experiment Association
AFSK: audio frequency-shift keying (modulation)
AM: amplitude modulation
AMA: Automatic message Accounting
ANI: Automatic Number Identification
ANSI: American National Standards Institute
API: application programming interface
ARPANET: Advanced Research Projects Agency Network
AT&T: American Telephone & Telegraph Company (AT&T)
ATM: automatic teller machine
Audion (triode): triode vacuum tube & amplifier, developed by Lee de Forest

BIS: Blackberry Internet Service
BISUP: Broadband ISDN User Part
BJT: bipolar junction transistor

C5: AT&T's predecessor to Signaling System 6; used for international calls
C6: European equivalent of Signaling System 6
C7: European equivalent of Signaling System 7
CAMA: centralized automatic message accounting
CAS: Channel Associated Signaling
CCI: call condition indicator
CCIS: Common Channel Interoffice Signaling
CCITT: Consultative Committee for International Telegraph and Telephone

CCS: Common Channel Signaling
CDMA: Code Division Multiple Access
CDR: call detail records
CLEC: competitive local exchange carrier
CMOS: complementary metal-oxide semiconductor
COLT: cell on light truck
COW: cell on wheels
CPU: central processing unit
CSAIL: MIT's Computer Science & Artificial Intelligence Laboratory
CSCF: Call Session Control Function
CTC: Copenhagen Telephone Company
CWDM: Coarse-Wavelength Division Multiplexing
CX: composite signaling

d-c: direct electric current
DDD: Direct Distance Dialing
DIAMETER: successor to RADIUS for AAA functions.
DSO-A: Common SS7 interface in North America
DTMF: dual-tone multi-frequency
DUP: Data User Part protocol
DWDM: Dense-Wavelength Division Multiplexing
DX: duplex signaling

ECSA: Exchange Carriers Standards Association
ESN: Electronic Serial Number
ESS: Electronic Switching system
ETSI: European Telecommunications Standards Institute

FCC: Federal Communications Commission
FiOS: Verizon branded bundled Internet access
FISU: Fill-In Signal Unit
FM: frequency modulation
FOTA: Firmware-Over-the-Air
FSK: frequency shift keying

GSC: Global Standards Collaborative
GSM: Global system for Mobiles
GTSC: Global Telecom Standards Collaborative (successor of GSC)

HLR: Home Location Register
HSS: Home Subscriber Server

Hz: hertz (radio frequency; equivalent to cycle per second)

IBSYS: circa 1960 IBM operating system derived from the predecessor system known as SHARE

iDEN: Integrated Digital Enhanced Network

IEEE: Institute of Electrical and Electronic Engineers, Inc.

IETF: Internet Engineering Task Force

ILEC: Incumbent Local Exchange Carrier

IMS: IP Multimedia Subsystem

IN: Intelligent Network

IP: Internet Protocol

IPSS: International Packet Switched Service

IR: infrared

ISDN: integrated Services Data Network

ISDN-UISO: International standards Organization

ISUP: ISDN User Part

ITSC: Inter-regional Standards Conference, is now defunct. The current organization is the Global Standards Collaboration.

ITU: International Telecommunication Union

ITU-D: ITU division with jurisdiction over telecommunications development

ITU-R: ITU division with jurisdiction over telecommunications radio matters

ITU-T: replaced earlier CCITT

IVR: Interactive Voice Response

LCR: Least Cost Routing

LNP: Local Number Portability

LRN: local Routing Number

LSSU: Line Status Signal Units

LTE: Long Term Evolution

M2PA: SIGTRAN-derived protocol to enable point-code IP connections between a signal gateway (SG) and a node, all routed outside of a TDM/SS7 environment.

M2UA: protocol developed for back haul of SS7 messages in an IP environment.

MAP: Mobile Access Part (OSI layer 6 or 7)

MDN: Mobile Directory Number

MEID: Mobile Electronic Identification Number

MF: multi-frequency

MFC: Multi-Frequency Compelled (e.g. R2 multi-frequency compelled signaling)
MG: media gateway
MGC: media gateway controller
MIN: Mobile Identification Number
MIT: Massachusetts Institute of Technology
MMS: Multimedia Messaging Service
MOS: Military Occupational Specialty
MSA: Metropolitan Statistics Area
MSC: Mobile (telephone) Switching Center
MSU: Message Signal Units
MTP: Message Transfer Part (SS7 protocol stack)
MTP1: Message Transfer Part 1 (physical level)
MTP2: Message Transfer Part 2 ((data link level)
MTP3 Message Transfer Part 3 (network level)
MTSO: Mobile Telephone Switching Office (aka MSC)
MWI: message waiting indicator

NPA: Numbering Plan Area(s)
NSF: National Science Foundation
NSFNET: National Science Foundation Network

OC1: OC (prefix) is a class of fiber optics cable
OEM: Original Equipment Manufacturer
OMAP: Operations, Maintenance and Administration Plan (in SS7)
OSI: Open System Interconnection
OTA: over-the-air (programming)

PBX: Private Branch Exchange
PCM: pulse code modulation
POTS: Pain Old Telephone Service
Project SCORE: Accomplished first U.S. broadcast from outer space
PSTN: Public Switched Telephone Network

Q.700: CCITT's 1980 publication entitled 'Introduction to CCITT SS7'
Q.701: CCITT Publication entitled "Functional Description of the Message Transfer Part'
Q.705: CCITT Publication entitled 'Signaling Network structure'
Q.710: CCITT Publication entitled 'PABX Application'

Q.780: CCITT Publication entitled 'SS No. 7 Test Specification (General)

Q.767: ITU-T document on international ISUP matters (1992)

R1: CCITT protocol that used MF tones in a CAS environment

R2: variation of MF signaling that used Multi-Frequency Compelled (MFC), as between a subscriber channel at a MTSO and a related digital signal processor.

RADIUS: Remote Authentication Dial In User Service

RBOC: Regional Bell Operating Companies

RBT: ringback tone

RCA: Radio Corporation of America

RF: radio frequency

ROM: Read Only Memory

RSSI: Received Signal Strength Indication

RTP: Real Time Protocol

SCCP: Signaling Connection Control Part

SCN: Switched Circuit Networks

SCORE: Communications satellite used in Operation SCORE

SCP: Service Control Point

SCTP: Stream Control Transmission Protocol

SEP: Signaling End Point (an SSP or a SCP)

SF: Status field (singe frequency)

SG: ITU study group prefix

SG11: ITU Study Group 11

SHARE: circa 1959 IBM operating system that was based on a General Motors predecessor

SIGSALY: top-secret encrypted signal system

SIGTRAN: Signaling Transport

SIP: Session Initiation Protocol

SMS: Short Message Service (text messages)

SMS: Service Management System

SNR: signal to noise ratio

SONET: Synchronous Optical Networking

SOS: poorly chosen acronym for SHARE Operating system

SPC: Stored Program Control (switch)

SS6: Signaling System 6

SS7: Signaling System 7

SSP: Service Switching Point

STP: Service Transfer Point

TC: termination code
TCAP: Transaction Capabilities Application Part
TCP: Transmission Control Protocol
TCP/IP: Transmission Control Protocol/Internet Protocol
TDM: Time Division Multiplexing
TIAA: Telecommunications Industry Association (of America)
TIROS I: Television Infrared Observation Satellite No. 1
TTC: Telecommunications Technology Committee (Japan)
TUP: Telephone User Part Protocol

UDP: User Datagram Protocol
UNI: User-network interface

V.35: high-speed data interface
VLR: Visited Location Register
VoIP: Voice over Internet Protocol
VPN: Virtual Private Network

WATS: Wide Area Telephone Service
WDM: Wavelength Division Multiplexing

X.25: Packet switched wide area network (WAN) protocol suite.

About the Author

Ralph Harvey [not to be confused with another author having the same name] writes primarily about civil and military aviation, history and technology. His interest in Signaling System 7 derived from a general interest in radio, radar and telecommunications, plus several years experience in technical support with a major telecom. A former transport pilot and adjunct college instructor, the author earned a Master of Science degree in manufacturing engineering from Worcester Polytechnic Institute.

Other books by Ralph Harvey:

Developing the Gull-Winged F4U Corsair – And Taking It To Sea

Man of the Waterfront: The Story of Kaye Williams and Captain's Cove

www.ingramcontent.com/pod-product-compliance
Lightning Source LLC
Chambersburg PA
CBHW052146070326
40689CB00050B/2341